SEDES SAPIENTIÆ

SEDES SAPIENTIÆ

—·◆·—

SPECIAL
ENGLISH-LANGUAGE
ISSUE N. 2

2024

AROUCA
PRESS

ISBN: 978-1-990685-97-2

Arouca Press
PO Box 55003
Bridgeport PO
Waterloo, ON N2J 0A5
Canada
www.aroucapress.com
Send inquiries to info@aroucapress.com

CONTENTS

FOREWORD

SEDES SAPIENTIÆ IS A QUARTERLY REVIEW published in French and dedicated to Christian formation. Founded more than thirty-five years ago by the Fraternity of St. Vincent Ferrer, it is placed under the protection of Our Lady, "Seat of Wisdom" (*Sedes Sapientiæ* in Latin) and of St. Thomas Aquinas. Its aim is to help Christians deepen their religious knowledge by forming their intellects in the light of the Common Doctor of the Church, St. Thomas Aquinas, and to contribute to religious debates in fidelity to the Tradition and magisterium of the Catholic Church.

In this second English-language issue of *Sedes Sapientiæ*, two prominent themes emerge. First, Fr. de Blignières and Joseph Shaw debate the feasibility of establishing an "ordinariate," i.e., a canonical structure with a bishop, to harbor traditional Catholics. This constructive solution to the current predicament of traditionalists stands in contrast to critical or defensive postures that "custodians of Tradition" have generally been constrained to adopt. Bishop Athanasius Schneider broaches the second principal theme of this issue, the religious life, with his personal testimony as a canon regular, which is complemented by a captivating portrait of the late Dominican friar, Fr. Tomáš Týn, by a Carmelite Sister.

Fr. Aidan Nichols, O. P., introduces the reader to a sharp discussion among Thomists on the sins of the angels. Noteworthy, too, is the somber reflection on Archbishop Lefebvre's 1988 consecrations co-written by two founders of *Ecclesia Dei* communities, as well as Fr. Reginald Rivoire's Thomistic exposition of "rationality" in canon law, which follows up on his highly acclaimed canonical analysis of *Traditionis custodes*. On a lighter note, the reader may alight upon an English lay-brother's whimsical commentary on the greatest of Chesterton's poems, or a review and chapter of the first English translation of the most ancient biography of St. Thomas Aquinas.

The world of faithful Catholics is continually tempted to conceive within itself the same intellectual disorder that it deplores in its adversaries. The formation of our minds has by now been principally entrusted, not to the eternal verities contained in old books, but to the ephemeral controversies flashing endlessly upon our monitors. Readers who have had the good fortune to lay hold of this issue of *Sedes Sapientiæ* will do their souls a good turn to read carefully the contents of this multifaceted collection, while pondering in their hands the most perfect technology that man will ever beget: the book.

Let us then extricate ourselves from every newfangled distraction to contemplate the old truths reclaimed in this new issue, dedicated to the Lady from whose womb the Wisdom of God made His dwelling among men.

David M. Foley, PhD
Fr. Antoine-Marie de Araujo, FSVF
Festo S. Anselmi MMXXIV

ACKNOWLEDGEMENTS

THE EDITORS WOULD LIKE TO THANK especially David M. Foley who proofread and corrected all the articles, and Alex Barbas of Arouca Press for helping us publish this second special issue in English. We are likewise thankful to John Pepino, Fr. Thomas Crean, O.P., Timothy Garvey, Philip Langton, Fr. William Barker, FSSP, and Bérengère Darlison, for their kind help.

Sedes Sapientiæ
Société Saint-Thomas-d'Aquin
53340 Chémeré-le-Roi
France

Tel.: (+33) 2 43 98 64 25
sedes@chemere.org
www.chemere.org

Religious Life
A MARIAN AND ANGELIC LIFE

BISHOP ATHANASIUS SCHNEIDER

Auxiliary Bishop of the Archdiocese of St. Mary in Astana

I N HIS *SUMMA THEOLOGIAE, ST.* THOMAS Aquinas defines religious life as follows:

> Wherefore those are called religious antonomas-tically, who give themselves up entirely to the divine service, as offering a holocaust to God. Hence Gregory says (*Hom. 20 in Ezech.*): "Some there are who keep nothing for themselves, but sacrifice to almighty God their tongue, their senses, their life, and the property they possess." Now the perfection of man consists in adhering wholly to God, as stated above (*ST* II-II, q. 184, a. 2), and in this sense religion denotes the state of perfection.[1]

The virtue of religion, the highest of the supernatural moral virtues, presides over the worship and service we owe to God, our sovereign Lord and Father. The religious or monastic life is the full realization of the virtue of religion, as St. Thomas Aquinas maintains:

> Accordingly, if a man devotes his whole life to the divine service, his whole life belongs to religion, and thus by reason of the religious life that they lead, those who are in the state of perfection are called religious.[2]

---

1   *ST* II-II, q. 186, a. 1, corp.
2   *ST* II-II, q. 186, a. 1, ad 2

RELIGIOUS LIFE IS A SCHOOL IN WHICH WE STRIVE FOR THE PERFECTION OF CHARITY.

St. Thomas Aquinas shows that the religious state of life is a "state of perfection" because it can lead souls to *perfect charity*. The perfection of Christian life is the perfect union with God, and this perfect union consists in perfect charity. As St. Thomas put it:

> A thing is said to be perfect in so far as it attains its proper end, which is the ultimate perfection thereof. Now it is charity that unites us to God, Who is the last end of the human mind, since "he that abideth in charity abideth in God, and God in him" (1 John 4:16). Therefore, the perfection of the Christian life consists radically in charity.[3]

The state of life specially directed to acquiring the perfection of charity, is thus called a "state of perfection." It is called *religious* life because it leads to the perfection of charity *through the perfection of the virtue of religion.*

By worshipping and serving God by religion, the highest supernatural moral virtue, consecrated persons can achieve perfect charity, the queen of the theological virtues.[4] Divine service leads to the intimacy of divine friendship in charity.[5] Indeed, according to St. Thomas, the virtue of religion makes one adhere (*inhaerere*) to God; and "religious," by putting all their acts at the service of God, truly direct all their acts towards this adhesion. When they pronounce the three vows of poverty, chastity and obedience, religious sacrifice all earthly goods to follow Christ in a special and radical way. The virtue

---

3   *ST* II-II, q. 184, a. 1, corp.

4   The virtue of charity is the most excellent of all the virtues: "Faith and hope attain God indeed in so far as we derive from Him the knowledge of truth or the acquisition of good, whereas charity attains God Himself that it may rest in Him, but not that something may accrue to us from Him. Hence charity is more excellent than faith or hope, and, consequently, than all the other virtues" (*ST* II-II, q. 23, a. 6, corp.).

5   Fr. Antoine Lemonnyer, French translation and commentary of *ST* II-II, q. 184ss, Collection "La Revue des Jeunes" (Paris: Cerf, 2010), 559.

of religion thus detaches the soul from all objects other than God. Now this detachment is also a detachment from that which hinders charity. Indeed, "the more a man is delivered from solicitude concerning temporal matters, the more perfectly he will be enabled to love God."[6] This is why devoting one's life to divine service is a most powerful way to acquire the perfection of charity.

In short, says St. Thomas Aquinas, "the religious state is a training school wherein one aims by practice at the perfection of charity."[7]

This humble and chaste state of life especially dedicated to serving and loving God has been compared to that of the angels and of the Blessed Virgin Mary.

Both in the Blessed Virgin Mary and in the holy Angels, humility and purity shine out most brilliantly. For this reason, the Blessed Virgin Mary and the holy Angels are, amongst creatures, the best models of a life of total dedication to the service of God.

THE MARIAN CHARACTER OF RELIGIOUS LIFE

Since the beginnings of the Church, the virginal Christian life has been linked to the example of the Blessed Virgin Mary.

Pope John Paul II admirably describes the Marian character of religious life in this way:

> Mary in fact is the *sublime example of perfect consecration,* since she belongs completely to God and is totally devoted to him. Chosen by the Lord, who wished to accomplish in her the mystery of the Incarnation, she reminds consecrated persons of *the primacy of God's initiative.* At the same time, having given her assent to the divine Word, made flesh in her, Mary is the *model of the acceptance of grace* by human creatures. Having lived with Jesus

---

6 St. Thomas Aquinas, *The Perfection of the Spiritual Life*, trans. John Procter, O. P. (St. Louis: B. Herder, 1902, and London: Sands, 1903), chapter VI. [https://isidore.co/aquinas/english].

7 *ST* II-II, q. 188, a. 1.

and Joseph in the hidden years of Nazareth, and
present at her Son's side at crucial moments of
his public life, the Blessed Virgin teaches unconditional discipleship and diligent service.[8]

This is why consecrated life looks to her as a sublime
model: accepting the "virginal and humble life of Christ
also means imitation of Mary's way of life."[9]

St. Alphonsus of Liguori left us some beautiful com-
ments regarding Our Lady's humility. Let us quote him
at length:

> Humility, says St. Bernard, is the foundation and
> guardian of the virtues; and with reason, for
> without it a soul can possess no other virtue. Let
> her possess all the virtues, they will all depart
> when humility departs. On the other hand, said
> St. Francis of Sales, in a letter to St. Jane de
> Chantal, God so loves humility that he instantly
> hastens to the soul in which he sees it. [...]
>
> The first act of humility of heart is to have an
> humble opinion of ourselves; and Mary always
> thought so lowly of herself, as was revealed
> to ... St. Matilda, that although she saw so many
> more graces bestowed upon her than upon others,
> she preferred all others before herself. Rupert
> the Abbot, explaining that passage, "Thou hast
> wounded my heart, my sister, my spouse with
> one hair of thy neck" (Cant. 4:9), says that this
> hair of the neck of the spouse was precisely that
> humble opinion which Mary had of herself, with
> which she wounded the heart of God. Not that
> the holy Virgin esteemed herself a sinner, for
> humility is truth, as St. Theresa says, and Mary
> knew that she had never offended God; nor that
> she did not confess having received greater graces
> from God than any other creature, for an humble
> heart always acknowledges the special favors of

---

8   Pope John Paul II, Apostolic Exhortation *Vita consecrata* (March
25, 1996), n. 28.
9   *Ibid.*

the Lord, that it may humble itself the more; but the divine mother, by the greater light she had to see the infinite greatness and goodness of her God, saw still more her own littleness, and therefore more than all others did she humiliate herself, and say with the spouse of the Canticles: "Do not consider that I am brown because the sun hath altered my color" (Cant. 1:6). Approaching him, I find myself black, as St. Bernard explains it: "*Appropinquans illi me nigram invenio.*" Yes, adds St. Bernardine, for the Virgin had always present before her eyes the divine majesty, and her own nothingness. As a beggar, when she is clothed with a costly garment which has been given her, is not made proud by it, but humbles herself more before the giver, because she is reminded then more of her poverty; thus, Mary, the more she saw herself enriched, the more humble she became, remembering that all was the gift of God; whence she herself said to St. Elizabeth, a Benedictine nun: "Know for certain that I esteemed myself most abject, and unworthy of the grace of God." And therefore, says St. Bernardine, no creature in the world has been more exalted, because no creature has ever humbled herself more than Mary.[10]

On the purity of the Blessed Virgin Mary, St. Louis Marie Grignion de Montfort said that "her divine purity has never had, and never can have, its equal under heaven."[11]

THE ANGELIC CHARACTER OF RELIGIOUS LIFE

The religious life has often been referred to by the Church Fathers as an "angelic life" (*bios angelikos*).

In their trial, the holy angels had to freely accept God

---

10   St. Alphonsus of Liguori, *The Glories of Mary*, New York: P. J. Kenedy & Sons, 1888), 594–597.
11   St. Louis Marie Grignion de Montfort, *Treatise on True Devotion to the Blessed Virgin*, Part II, IV (London: Catholic Way Publishing, 2013), 119.

in deep humility. The sin of the first of the angels, known in tradition as Lucifer, was that he wanted to be like God but without God, as St. Thomas Aquinas explains:

> [Lucifer] desired resemblance with God ... by desiring, as his last end of beatitude, something which he could attain by the virtue of his own nature, turning his appetite away from supernatural beatitude, which is attained by God's grace. Or, if he desired as his last end that likeness of God which is bestowed by grace, he sought to have it by the power of his own nature; and not from Divine assistance according to God's ordering.[12]

With this act of pride, Lucifer influenced part of the angelic world and took it with him in his fall.

Many theologians have put forward the hypothesis that the mystery of the divine Incarnation was revealed to the angels and that they saw how a nature inferior to their own was to be hypostatically united to the person of God the Son, so that the whole hierarchy of heaven should bow down to adore the majesty of the Incarnate Word. This, it is supposed, was the cause of Lucifer's pride.[13] It is very likely that God revealed the mystery of the Incarnation to them so that they would prostrate themselves and serve the Incarnate God. They had to agree to serve God not only in His majesty, but also in a veiled and hidden form as the future incarnate God-Man. To this, the first angel replied: "No, I will not do that. I will not serve. *Non serviam!* I will not serve and I will not bow down in contempt of my dignity to serve a man. I want to be like God." The famous German neo-scholastic theologian Matthias Scheeben († 1888) declared that the link between the mystery of the Incarnation and the fall of the angels provides a plausible and even probable

---

12   *ST* I, q. 63, a. 3, corp.
13   Cf. Suárez, *De Angelis*, lib. 7, cap. 13, *Opera omnia* (Paris: Vives, 1866) tom. 2, 880–889.

explanation for the intensity of the devil's detestation of Christ, the Blessed Virgin Mary and the human race.

According to tradition, the pride of Lucifer and his followers was so strong that they preferred their ego—"I am I," said Lucifer. Then, in the midst of this trial, one of the humblest angels, St. Michael, who belonged to the penultimate choir, said: "*Quis ut Deus?*" With these humble words, St. Michael threw Lucifer and all his followers from heaven into the abyss. My guardian angel and all the guardian angels remained faithful to God in this trial; they accepted Christ in a spirit of humility and service.

Therefore, we can think that, since then, the most fervent desire of every angel is to one day become a humble guardian angel and the servant of a human being. Every angel ardently desires this. Every angel's "career plan" is to prostrate himself. His "dream career" is to be small, to descend, and not to ascend, as is the ambition of human beings for their own careers. We human beings, with the wounds of original sin, including pride, desire to pursue a career and occupy high positions. The opposite is true of the holy angels. What they desire in their careers is to descend. So, for example, when a cherub becomes a guardian angel for a limited time in a person's life, he descends from the second choir to the ninth. He is stripped and reduced to the dignity of the lowest choir, and it is his deepest desire to be at the very bottom, to imitate Christ his Lord, to be a servant. Consequently, the ambition of every angel is to one day be a guardian angel, to experience the lowliness of the last angelic choir and to be at the humble and patient service of an individual human person.

The favorite prayer of the holy angels is the "*Sanctus.*" The essence of each angel says: "God is holy and God alone is holy and God is great." The holy angels burn to praise and glorify God. We must ask them to give us some of their humility, their burning fire, their sacred zeal for the glory of God.

A 19th century spiritual author, Archbishop W. B. Ullathorne, writes of humility:

It would take many volumes to repeat what the Fathers and Saints have written in exposition and enforcement of this their favorite virtue. The chief points on which they dwell are these: 1. That humility is the distinctive virtue of Christ, and of the true Christian. 2. That it is the very groundwork of sanctity and salvation. 3. That it is the essential condition upon which the divine gifts are received. 4. That it is the mother and the nurse of the virtues. 5. That the depth of humility measures the greatness of the gifts received by the soul. 6. That the more they strove with great labour to cultivate this virtue, the nearer they found themselves to God, and were the more amazed to see how little it was understood or prized among Christians, except those who aspired to perfection. 7. In short, that the want of steady and persevering labour in this virtue was the cause of all failures in the supernatural life.[14]

The holy angels are also an eminent model of purity and chastity, and an effective help in leading a virginal and chaste life. An old catechism says that those who lead a chaste life resemble the angels and are most pleasing in God's sight:

Those whose life is pure are angels in human form. Chastity is an angelic virtue; by it men become like the angels. Chaste souls are in fact superior to the angels, because they have the flesh to combat, which the angels have not; they preserve angelic purity in spite of the continual temptations of the devil. What differentiates the angels from men is not their virtue, but their bliss. The purity of the angels is more blissful; that of man is stronger because it is the result of struggle. We learn from the lives of the saints

---

14   Archbishop W. B. Ullathorne, *The Groundwork of the Christian Virtues*, 7th ed. (London: Burns & Oates, no date), 230–231.

that angels delight in the company of chaste mortals, thus proving that they regard them as their equals. The devils know that through chastity man recovers the angelic dignity which he lost, hence they strive assiduously to instill impure thoughts into his mind. [Persons] who live chastely are extremely pleasing to God. Christ when on earth showed a predilection for chaste souls; He chose a pure virgin for His Mother, a man of angelic purity for His foster-father; the Baptist, who was purified in his mother's womb, was His precursor; the chaste John was His favorite disciple, privileged at the Last Supper to rest upon His breast; at the foot of the cross two pure souls stood; and He loved little children because of their innocence. "He that loveth cleanness of heart shall have the King for his friend" (Prov. 2:11). God calls the chaste soul by the endearing title of friend, of sister, of spouse (Cant. 4:6–8).[15]

Pope Pius XII echoes the traditional comparison between the religious and the angels in his Encyclical *Sacra virginitas*:

Virginity fully deserves the name of angelic virtue, which St. Cyprian writing to virgins affirms: "What we are to be, you have already commenced to be. You already possess in this world the glory of the resurrection; you pass through the world without suffering its contagion. In preserving virgin chastity, you are the equals of the angels of God." To souls, restless for a purer life or inflamed with the desire to possess the kingdom of heaven, virginity offers itself as "a pearl of great price," for which one "sells all that he has, and buys it" (Mt. 13:46). Married people and even those who are captives of vice, at the contact of virgin souls, often admire the splendor

15   Francis Spirago, *The Catechism Explained*, 9th ed. (New York: Benziger Brothers, 1899) 500–501 (https://openlibrary.org/books/OL7055928M/The_catechism_explained).

of their transparent purity, and feel themselves
moved to rise above the pleasures of sense. When
St. Thomas states "that to virginity is awarded
the tribute of the highest beauty," it is because
its example is captivating; and, besides, by their
perfect chastity do not all these men and women
give a striking proof that the mastery of the spirit
over the body is the result of a divine assistance
and the sign of proven virtue?[16]

It is important to stress that being like angels does not
mean despising their body or marriage. God created the
joys of human love, marriage and the family; in themselves,
these are very precious goods, objects of legitimate desire.
This is precisely why these goods can be "sold" in order
to "buy" an even more precious good: the Kingdom of
Heaven. Thus consecrated virginity, although a *sacrifice*, is
truly a "good deal."

As mentioned earlier, since angels have no body, they do
not even practice purity or chastity in the physical sense
of the word. For them, chastity means choosing God alone,
once and for all, irrevocably. Their life is "purely" oriented
towards divine service. Likewise, religious renounce the
legitimate goods of marriage and family life in order to
dedicate themselves entirely to the service of the Lord.
Here "purity" means preventing any human love from
distracting them from love for God, following St. Paul's
advice to the Corinthians (1 Cor. 7:32–35):

> But I would have you without carefulness. He
> that is unmarried careth for the things that
> belong to the Lord, how he may please the Lord:
> But he that is married careth for the things that
> are of the world, how he may please his wife.
> There is difference also between a wife and a
> virgin. The unmarried woman careth for the
> things of the Lord, that she may be holy both
> in body and in spirit: but she that is married

---

16   Pope Pius XII, Encyclical *Sacra virginitas* (March 25, 1954), n. 29.

careth for the things of the world, how she may please her husband.

Religious sacrifice human affections and procreation to focus their power of loving on God only, as explained in the *Code of Canon Law* (can. 599):

> The evangelical counsel of chastity assumed for the sake of the kingdom of heaven, which is a sign of the world to come and a source of more abundant fruitfulness in an undivided heart, entails the obligation of perfect continence in celibacy.

THE PRACTICE OF PERFECT CHASTITY ACCORDING TO PIUS XII

Consecrated virginity is a difficult virtue that requires strong and noble souls to do battle and conquer for the sake of the Kingdom of Heaven. This is especially true in our times when chastity in general and consecrated virginity in particular are often under attack. Addressing religious in *Sacra virginitas*, Pope Pius XII emphasizes that God gives consecrated persons the necessary graces to remain faithful:

> And yet, although chastity pledged to God is a difficult virtue, those who after serious consideration generously answer Christ's invitation and do all in their power to attain it, can perfectly and faithfully preserve it. For since they have eagerly embraced the state of virginity or celibacy, they will certainly receive from God that gift of grace through whose help they will be able to carry out their promise.[17]

Pius XII then gives some practical advice on how to keep the virtue of chastity. (These instructions, although intended for religious, are useful in any state of life). Let us summarize them in six points.

---

17 Pope Pius XII, *Sacra virginitas*, n. 51.

First, one should never forget that chastity is a gift of God, and hence we should constantly *pray* to receive such a grace. The Pope quotes three Doctors of the Church to support his point:

> Jerome wrote these succinct words: "It is given to those who have asked for it, who have desired it, who have worked to receive it. For it will be given to everyone who asks, the seeker will find, to the importunate it will be opened" (*Comm. in Matth.*, 19, 11). Ambrose adds that the constant fidelity of virgins to their Divine Spouse depends upon prayer (*De virginibus*, 3, 4). [...] St. Alphonsus Liguori taught that there is no help more necessary and certain for conquering temptations against the beautiful virtue of chastity than instant recourse to God in prayer (*Practica di amar Gesu Cristo*, c. 17, nn. 7–16).

Since we also draw the grace of God from the *sacraments*, the Holy Father recommends "frequent and fervent use of the Sacrament of Penance which, as a spiritual medicine, purifies and heals us"; and he invites us to receive the Eucharist, "the best remedy against lust."

Second, chastity involves a *struggle* to avoid the temptations of the flesh. Pius XII urges those who vow chastity to "watch particularly over the movements of their passions and of their senses," and also to practice "bodily mortification" in order to "render them obedient to right reason and God's law," so that the soul can reign fully over the body.[18]

Thirdly, because of human weakness, one of the best ways to win the spiritual combat against impurity is simply *to avoid* it.

> For the preserving of chastity, according to the teaching of Jerome, flight is more effective than open warfare: "Therefore I flee, lest I be overcome" (*Contra Vigilant.*, 16). Flight must be

---

18   *Ibid.*, n. 36.

understood in this sense, that not only do we diligently avoid occasion of sin, but especially that in struggles of this kind we lift our minds and hearts to God.... "Look upon the beauty of your Lover," St. Augustine tells us (*De sancta virginitate*, 54).[19]

One aspect of this courageous flight is called *modesty*:

[Modesty] does not like impure or loose talk, it shrinks from the slightest immodesty, it carefully avoids suspect familiarity with persons of the other sex, since it brings the soul to show due reverence to the body, as being a member of Christ and the temple of the Holy Spirit.[20]

Humility is perhaps the most necessary virtue for the protection of consecrated virginity, lest such a great gift of God be corrupted by pride.

Finally, Pius XII's last advice sums up all the others, and helps us see how religious life is a *Marian* life:

The eminent way to protect and nourish an unsullied and perfect chastity [...] is solid and fervent devotion to the Virgin Mother of God. In a certain way all other helps are contained in this devotion; there is no doubt that whoever is sincerely and earnestly animated by this devotion is salutarily inspired to constant vigilance, to continual prayer, to receive the Sacraments of Penance and the Holy Eucharist. Therefore in a paternal way We exhort all priests, religious men and women, to entrust themselves to the special protection of the holy Mother of God who is the Virgin of virgins and the "teacher of virginity," as Ambrose says, and the most powerful Mother of those in particular who have vowed and consecrated themselves to the service of God.[21]

---

19 *Ibid.*, n. 54.
20 *Ibid.*, n. 58.
21 *Ibid.*, n. 64.

John Paul II echoed this teaching when he said that consecrated persons, in a special way, can consider the Blessed Virgin Mary as their Mother.

> Indeed, if the new motherhood conferred on Mary at Calvary is a gift for all Christians, it has a specific value for those who have completely consecrated their lives to Christ. "Behold your mother!" (Jn. 19:27): Jesus' words to the disciple "whom he loved" (Jn. 19:26) are particularly significant for the lives of consecrated persons. They, like John, are called to take the Blessed Virgin Mary to themselves (cf. Jn. 19:27), loving her and imitating her in the radical manner which befits their vocation, and experiencing in return her special motherly love. The Blessed Virgin shares with them the love which enables them to offer their lives every day for Christ and to cooperate with him in the salvation of the world. Hence a filial relationship to Mary is the royal road to fidelity to one's vocation and a most effective help for advancing in that vocation and living it fully.[22]

CONCLUSION

Every person consecrated to God in the state of religious life must strive day by day more and more for the virtues of humility and chastity of body and heart, and in this way lead a more Marian and angelic life, that is, according to the example of the Blessed Virgin Mary and the holy Angels.

---

22   Pope John Paul II, *Vita consecrata*, n. 28.

Questions to Bishop Athanasius Schneider on Religious Life

Excellency, are you yourself a religious?

I belong to the Order of the Canons Regular of the Holy Cross, the order I joined in 1982 at the age of twenty-one. The Canons Regular follow the Rule of St. Augustine. As Bishop of Hippo, St. Augustine insisted that his clergy living at his cathedral should live under a common rule and hold no private property. The charism of the Canons Regular consists in the "apostolic life," in the living both a contemplative and pastorally active life. The Canons Regular consider the solemn liturgy as their primary task. The Order to which I belong was founded in 1132 in Coimbra with the title of the "Holy Cross." St. Anthony of Padua was a member of this Order and received his theological formation and priestly ordination at Coimbra before he passed to the Order of the Friars Minor. The Co-founder and first Prior General of the Order the Canons Regular of the Holy Cross was St. Theotonius († 1162), the first canonized saint of Portugal.

What did it mean for you to pronounce perpetual vows of poverty, chastity and obedience?

To pronounce the three perpetual vows of poverty, chastity and obedience meant for me a total consecration of my person and of all aspects of the human and Christian life exclusively to the Lord. It meant for me a solemn declaration that from now on the Lord is the owner, the king and ruler of my soul, my heart, my body and all that I possess. I had the sensation of a deep and unspeakable happiness to belong in a spousal way forever to the Lord. The life of consecrated poverty, chastity and obedience is the fullest expression of the imitation of Christ. When you love Jesus Christ really and supernaturally, you have the desire to be like Him. The secret of holiness consists in continuously striving to be like Christ through chaste thoughts, desires, and a chaste body, through a life of complete detachment from material things and above all through detachment from self-will. The perpetual vows were for me summarized and expressed in the Latin adage: *Totus tuus ego sum, et omnia mea tua sunt* ("I totally belong to You, and all that I have is Yours").

Is religious life still necessary to the Church in our times? It could seem more urgent to promote priestly vocations and to defend the holiness of Christian marriage.

All three realities are in their own way necessary for the life of the Church. If any of these three realities were missing, something essential for the Church would be missing. All three are interdependent, one on the other. The first reality of the Church is the Catholic family, sanctified through the sacrament of marriage and the example of the Holy Family. The Catholic family is in a way the first priestly seminary. Without the priesthood the Church cannot live, because without the Eucharist, which priests alone are able to consecrate validly, there is no life in the Church, since she lives from the Eucharist. Without religious life there will be lacking the perpetual flame of spousal love for Christ and the most eloquent witness to the primacy of eternity.

What practical advice would you give to young people who are thinking of consecrating themselves to God?

The desire of consecrating themselves to God which arises in the souls of young persons comes from God. It is a tactful invitation from God to this individual young person to love, to love unreservedly the Supreme Good,

God Himself. It is first of all a gift from God. As soon as a young person feels such a desire, he or she must follow it, imploring from God the grace of strengthening this desire and of remaining faithful to this call. Then one should humbly pray that God may grant definite signs which will indicate the place or the form of consecrated life, to which God from all eternity decided to call him. Young people should seek those religious communities where the consecrated life is lived in full, and to a certain extent in radical observance and traditional ascesis, combined with serenity and joy. This means those religious communities where God is given the first place through the primacy of prayer, a Christocentric and sacred form of celebrating the liturgy, and through an ardent desire to save souls for eternity and build up the missionary life of the Church. An authentic religious, whether male or female, is a true and effective missionary. The secret of a truly fulfilling religious life consists in not losing one's first love (cf. Rev. 2:4), but rather doing everything in order to nurture it.

FR. TOMÁŠ TÝN, O.P. (1950–1990)

"He was like a diamond"

THE LIFE OF THE SERVANT OF GOD FATHER TOMÁŠ TÝN, O.P.

A CARMELITE SISTER IN ENGLAND

O N MAY 3, 1950, TOMÁŠ JOSEPH Maria Týn, eldest son of Ludmila Konupcikova, a neuropsychiatrist, and Zdenek Týn, a psychiatrist, was born in Brno, in what was then Czechoslovakia, now the Czech Republic. Tomáš was followed by a sister, Helena, and by Pavel, the youngest son. The name Tomáš was prophetically given to him in honour of St. Thomas Aquinas, towards whom his parents had a special devotion on account of a course of spiritual exercises preached by Dominicans which the Týn couple had had the grace to follow. The Týn family was heroically faithful to the Christian principles in which they educated little Tomáš, and they put up a strong resistance to the Communist system and to the atheism of the regime.

THE EARLY YEARS

From an early age Tomáš, brought up largely by his maternal grandmother, Vilemina, a profoundly Catholic woman, and his great-aunt, Maria Ritschl, a highly cultured person who lived with the Týn family, showed uncommon intellectual gifts combined with intense piety. He attended Mass with great reverence and served as an altar boy, becoming very familiar not only with the ceremonies but also with the texts of the Mass.

In 1959, he made his First Holy Communion. Afterwards, the family went on an outing to enjoy the beauties of nature. It was a happy occasion during which the whole family felt united, but at one point Tomáš suddenly turned to his younger sister and said: "Remember, Helena, *morte vita non tollitur, sed mutatur* ('by death life is changed, not taken away')."[1] The family never forgot it. Tomáš was then 10 or 11 years old, but already showed deep piety and an unusual insight into divine things. It is not surprising, then, that at about the age of 15, he felt God's call, saying: "I will become a priest and a religious." According to some witnesses, though, his vocation dated back a few years earlier.

COMMUNISM AND THE SECULARIZED WEST

Thanks to a scholarship that he received for his excellent marks at school, Tomáš went to study in Dijon, France. This experience of the secularized West surprised and deeply distressed the young student. He observed, remarks R. Schinco, that

> Western peoples, instead of building a strong and healthy civil and social structure, in accordance with the principles of the Catholic tradition, were suffering the influences of propaganda from beyond the Iron Curtain, thanks to the so-called fifth column, and were allowing themselves to be fascinated by those same Marxist ideologies, for which he had already suffered so much in his homeland. Before his eyes, protests, social unrest, strikes and violent demonstrations were becoming more and more frequent, involving young students ever more intensely and culminating in the events of 1968, which he described as 'a year terrible to the memory.' It was a harsh disillusionment for this enthusiastic and optimistic young Czechoslovakian.[2]

---

1   *Missale Romanum*, Preface for the Dead.
2   R. Schinco (ed.), *La Beata sempre Vergine Maria Madre di Dio. Omelie Mariane del Servo di Dio Padre Tomas Tyn O.P* (Faenza, 2009), 25.

He had come to know Communism well in his home-land and had understood how completely incompatible are Marx's philosophy and the Gospel.

Being naturally sociable and communicative, Tomáš was always friendly toward his companions, but he carefully avoided anything that might even slightly tarnish the angelic purity that had always characterized him and that marked him out as a chosen son of St. Dominic.

In the summer of 1968, back in Brno for his holidays, Tomáš saw the Soviet tanks invading the city, to the terror and dismay of the inhabitants. Although he was only 18 years old, he was already sufficiently mature for this terrifying sight, at once a symbol and a culmination of Communist totalitarianism, to lead him later, on the day of his priestly ordination, to offer his life for the freedom of his homeland. He attributed his vocation to the fight against Communism, as he recalled during a homily on Fatima in 1987: "It is to Communism that I owe my religious vocation, and may the Lord be blessed and thanked."

IN GERMANY, AS A SON OF ST. DOMINIC

In France, on July 1, 1969, Tomáš received his bachelor's degree with outstanding grades. It was during this time that he met the Dominican Father Henri-Marie Féret, an eminent theologian, who confirmed him in his religious and priestly vocation, and directed him towards the Dominican Order. During his time in France, Tomáš learned several languages well: Russian, French, German, Hebrew, Greek and Latin. Meanwhile, in 1968, following the Soviet invasion, his parents left Czechoslovakia and took refuge in West Germany.

After leaving France, Tomáš joined his family in Germany, where, on September 28, 1969, he took the habit of the Order of Preachers in Warburg, Westphalia. Here he began his novitiate, which ended on September 29 of the following year, with his temporary profession. He then began his philosophical and theological studies in the studium in Walberberg, in the Dominican Province of Teutonia. Here he received a lectorate in sacred theology, writing a thesis on *La problematica del moto e della quiete secondo Platone* ("The Problem of Motion and Rest according to Plato").

But this was the time just after the Second Vatican Council, and the winds of novelty were unfortunately blowing through most religious houses. This was especially true in Germany, where the innovations that followed the Council were turning into a veritable revolution. It is not hard to see how the consequent relaxation of religious life, along with the wish to "get rid of tradition" in matters of doctrine, would contrast grievously with the yearning of the young friar after evangelical purity. But Tomáš had heard that the Dominicans in Bologna wanted to apply the conciliar texts in continuity with the perennial tradition of the Church. And so, in 1972, he asked and obtained permission to go to Italy, to the Dominican Province of Bologna, where the relics of St. Dominic are preserved. It was here that Brother Tomáš took his perpetual vows on July 19, 1973 and was ordained deacon on November 26 of the same year. In the meantime, he obtained his licentiate in theology with a thesis in Latin entitled *De gratia divina et iustificatione. Oppositio inter theologiam Sancti Thomae et Lutheri* ("On divine grace and justification: The opposition between the theology of St. Thomas and Luther"), under the direction of Father Alberto Galli, a fervent soul and a thoroughgoing Thomist.

This thesis already reveals the love for truth of this exceptional son of St. Dominic. While examining the relationship between grace and free will according to Thomistic doctrine, he unmasks and refutes the impostures of the neo-Modernists who tend to accept Protestant errors in a Catholic guise. In particular, he refutes Karl Rahner who, according to Father Týn, "fell into theological errors by accepting falsehoods in philosophy." He explains: "Every error of modernism comes from being unable to balance human reason and the truth of faith, and so falling either into an irrational traditionalism or into an exaggerated rationalism." Father Tomáš had fully understood that at the root of an erroneous theology there is always a no less erroneous philosophy. He remained until the end "a fierce opponent of Marxism and Communism, whose very serious fundamental errors he denounced with impeccable reasoning as destructive of religion, human dignity, the value of the moral law and the good of society."[3]

The young friar's apostolic life in Bologna was intense, though his community life was not easy. On the latter, however, as also on his own interior life, this extraordinary Dominican spread a veil of silence. "True courage," he said, "does not mean denying difficulties, but facing them with the help of our holy Catholic faith"; and again: "Through the joy that comes to us from Christ the Savior, we are able, with God, to overcome everything."

SACERDOS IN ÆTERNUM

On June 29, 1975, Brother Tomáš was ordained a priest by Pope Paul VI. "Those who are consecrated are not consecrated *ad tempus*, but *usque ad perpetuam æternitatem*," Father Týn would remark in 1987. In a homily on the Presentation in the Temple of the Blessed Virgin Mary he said: "Even after death, persons who have been consecrated continue to be so." — "This total and definitive choice implies the necessity of sacrifice, since it is a choice of the love of God, of the love of God above all else, and whoever belongs to God cannot belong to himself."[4] The new priest faithfully fulfilled his own words, for on that day, as became known after his death, he offered his life secretly and in silence for the freedom of the Church in his homeland, devastated as it was by the Communist regime.

---

3   G. Cavalcoli, O. P., "Tomáš Tyn, Un dissidente della ex-Cecoslovacchia" (Bologna, 2008). Available online at: http://www.studiodomenicano.com/testi/Padre_Tomas_Tyn,_un_dissidente_della_ex-Cecoslovacchia.pdf.

4   R. Schinco, *La Beata sempre Vergine Maria*, 31.

After his ordination to the priesthood, Father Tomáš studied at the Angelicum in Rome where, in 1978, he obtained his doctorate in Theology with a thesis on "Divine action and human freedom in the process of justification according to the doctrine of St. Thomas Aquinas," returning to the theme he had treated in his licentiate, but this time focusing only on St. Thomas.

CONTEMPLARI ET CONTEMPLATA ALIIS TRADERE

From 1978 until his premature death, Father Týn carried out exemplary apostolic work in Bologna, according to the Dominican ideal, *contemplari et contemplata aliis tradere*.[5] In 1980 he became Professor as well as Vice-Moderator of Moral Theology at the Studio Teologico Accademico Bolognese (STAB); in 1984, he became a member of the Province's Commission for Intellectual Life; and in 1989, Vice-Moderator of the St. Dominic Section of the STAB. In addition to teaching at the Tincani Institute, he also preached for associations such as Alleanza Cattolica, as well as in universities, to boy scouts, and to non-believers, including Jews. Added to this was the ministry of confession and spiritual direction, as well as retreats and lectures given in various places. His great purity of life also enabled him to do much work among female religious. These included the Dominican nuns of Fontanellato and Castel San Pietro, the Sisters of Blessed Imelda, the contemplative nuns of St. Agnes, the oldest community in Bologna, and the community in Via Palestro.

"The methodical wisdom with which he knew how to spend his time," wrote one of his brethren,

> along with his great virtues and natural gifts, enabled him, in his brief life, to achieve results remarkable for both quality and quantity. They ranged from the most abstract theology to the most wide-ranging and various kinds of pastoral

---

5 "To contemplate and to give to others the fruits of one's contemplation": Cf. *ST* II-II, q. 188, a. 6, corp.

and priestly ministry among people of all ages, classes, and social, economic and educational backgrounds. He had a special love for children, and photographs show him among them happy and smiling much more than among learned persons, with whom he nevertheless conversed easily, thanks to his great culture. However, he never allowed his talents to make him at all burdensome to other people. Rather he concealed them, by a kind of irony, not wanting to seem like a know-it-all and so as not to humiliate "the little ones."[6]

Much useful evidence remains of his varied apostolate in Bologna. There are cyclostyled notes for his lectures at the STAB and articles published in the paper "St. Dominic on Tuesday" and elsewhere. Naturally, as a good theologian, he also published in specialist journals. Added to this are numerous recordings of him speaking. It is here that "Father Tomáš's incomparable oratorical skills" appear. He would speak without a text, and before he began to teach he would immerse himself deeply in prayer. However, his masterpiece was the treatise *La Metafisica della Sostanza. Partecipazione e* Analogia Entis ("The Metaphysics of Substance: Participation and the Analogy of Being"), a work written in the midst of a feverish apostolate, and finished in the last months of his life, when sufferings had begun to wear out his hitherto robust constitution.[7]

A SOUL ON FIRE

What was most attractive about this young Dominican, and which explains the success of his apostolate, was his lack of compromise. He loved truth in all its purity and made no compromises whenever it was called into question. "The word of the Lord," he said, "cannot be altered and

---

6   G. Cavalcoli, O. P., "Vita e opere di Tomas Tyn," (Bologna, 2008). Available online at: http://www.studiodomenicano.com/testi/Vita_e_opere_di_Tomas_Tyn.pdf.

7   Cf. R. Schinco, *La Beata sempre Vergine Maria*, 33–35.

remains for ever. It is better to be few but faithful than
to be many but sometimes unfaithful." We read again in
his Homilies:

> I judge no one. I judge how things are: social
> collapse, de-Christianisation, desecration. Why
> has life in society become unliveable? Because it
> is no longer Christian: having no Christian soul
> and no grace, it has no humanity. Without God,
> man cannot be man! This is a first principle of
> theological anthropology, of any anthropology
> that does not want to be bestial. [....] I do not
> want shortcuts to happiness; I prefer the way
> of the saints.[8]

He was intransigent towards the 'pacificism' that spread
everywhere after Vatican II. He denounced it in such
words as these:

> Dear brothers, God's action is truly a two-edged
> sword. I know how easy it is today to follow
> that pseudo-pacifist intellectual movement that
> does not like swords of any kind, and least of
> all the sword of God. But this is how things are:
> God with the sword of His almighty word has
> severed darkness from light.... You see, Gnosti-
> cism—which is the rebellion of man that copies
> the rebellion of Satan, since Satan was the first
> Gnostic—consists in this: not recognising the
> difference between ourselves and God, not recog-
> nising that light is separated from darkness: you
> see, it wants to mix light and darkness together.[9]

Despite his numerous apostolic commitments, Father
Tomáš followed religious and political events closely, both
in Italy and elsewhere, convinced that there is no separation between the spiritual and temporal order and that
Christianity must permeate the whole of society with its

---

8   Roberto de Mattei, "P. Tomas Tyn 30 anni dopo: un domenicano
senza compromessi," *Radici cristiane*, n. 33 (April 2008): 53–55.
9   T. Týn, "Omelia su Maria Santissima in tempo pasquale," in R.
Schinco, *La Beata sempre Vergine Maria*, 71.

truth. He criticized certain political actions of the Holy See respectfully but firmly, such as the *détente* towards Communist regimes and the concordat made with the Italian state in 1985. Father Tomáš did not approve of the policy of the Vatican's Secretary of State, Cardinal Agostino Casaroli, which was to reach agreements with the Czech Communist regime about the appointment of bishops. He was convinced that it would be better to have no bishops than to have Casaroli's agreed bishops. We should frankly recognize today that both history and theology show this judgement to have been prophetic.[10]

In regard to Communism, he was always unyielding. When, in the 1980s, a group of counter-revolutionary activists demonstrated outside Bologna's churches, seeking to alert Catholics to what was at stake, and using the slogan "Against Communism and Against Abortion," Father Týn joined them with his characteristic simplicity and courage. He also clashed with Father Michele Casali, O. P., when the latter invited Alexander Dubcek for a conference organized by the St. Dominic Centre, and asked Father Týn to act as interpreter.[11] Father Týn refused even to meet Dubcek, on the grounds that, despite the latter's opposition to Soviet dominance, he was still a Communist.

In a lecture given to a religious community, he said bluntly: "These masters of the East, these people who are in power in the countries where Satan reigns, have no desire for truth, no desire at all, and the Vatican knows it. So you can see how harmful any openness to these gentlemen, or any dialogue with them, would be." Along the same lines, his homily of November 7, 1987 is still famous. It was the 70th anniversary of the Bolshevik Revolution,

---

10   Cf. R. de Mattei, "P. Tomas Tyn 30 anni dopo".
11   Alexander Dubcek was a Czechoslovak politician (1921–1992). He took part in the Communist resistance, and was a member of the Presidium and Secretary of the Communist Party of Czechoslovakia from 1963 to 1968. He led an era of political liberalization known as the Prague Spring. During this period, he carried out a series of reforms in order to establish a "socialism with a human face."

and Father Tomáš wished to celebrate Mass *pro defensione Ecclesiae suae*, with purple vestments, because—as he said in a voice of thunder—"today is a day of exultation for the wicked, but for the good it must be a day of mourning and penitence." In this homily, he recalled Pope Pius XI's encyclical *Divini Redemptoris*, in which, as he remarked:

> The Pope affirms that the Communist system rests on a false idea of redemption;...Communism is not a system of philosophy, it is not a system of social ethics; it is a counter-church and a counter-religion.... The word Counter-church indicates that Communism is essentially atheistic, it is not so *per accidens*...Communism is essentially, intrinsically perverse...I hear it said today that there is one kind of Communism that is godless, and another that is good and acceptable. That, brothers, is disastrous! Let no one be deceived: Communism is intrinsically perverse and to collaborate with it in any area of life is unlawful.

In regard to the controversial case of Cardinal Mindszenty, Father Tomáš stated:

> The Vatican, it must be said very frankly, has unfortunately lost its credibility with the good Catholics of that country by replacing him with another prelate. It is quite straightforward: where we come from, people are not stupid, they know how to tell the difference between the clergy who remain faithful to the Apostolic See and the national clergy, i.e., the separatist, schismatic clergy, the national churches, which of course their Communist masters want to impose on the Church in order to detach it from Rome.

And he concluded: "This is what comes of Ostpolitik."[12]

Nor did he spare the progressivism rampant in the human element of the Church of God:

---

12   T. Týn, "La Chiesa postconciliare," May 1985.

> If the "singular wild boar of the forest" wreaks
> a very obvious devastation, the little foxes also
> work their devastation, going about the vineyard
> and gnawing in whatever way they can at the
> roots of the mystical vine. You see, dear brothers,
> there are modernists who want to bring about a
> separation of the faith from its roots in Christ.
> Well then: what must we do? Let neither the
> wild boar of the forest, nor the little foxes, which
> are so hard to see, ravage the mystical vineyard
> of the Lord. [13]

Nevertheless, he combined this firmness and constancy
of principle with a great charity for souls, even the most
misguided. "Father Tomáš knew how to distinguish error
from the person who erred: although he was uncompro-
mising towards error, he had great charity for people,
so much so that he was able to bring even atheists and
other non-believers closer to the Church. His apostolate was all-embracing: from the extreme right to the
extreme left." [14]

In a tribute written shortly after his death, one of
his brothers said of him very aptly: "He was like a dia-
mond!"—an allusion both to the purity of his life and to
the orthodoxy of his thought.

LIFE OF PENANCE

Father Tomáš' learning was immense. He read with
unusual speed and so was able to commit to memory
philosophical writings of all periods and kinds, as well as
texts from the other branches of human knowledge. Yet
his apostolic activity was impressive as well, and it wore
a distinctly penitential aspect.

In a homily on the Feast of Our Lady of Lourdes,
Father Tomáš said, faithfully repeating the words of the
Immaculate Virgin: "We must do penance"; and again:

---

13   G. Cavalcoli, O. P., "Tomas Tyn, Un dissidente della ex-Cecoslovacchia."
14   *Ibid.*

"For mankind today, with its pseudo-angelic pride, with its quest for the superman, penance is so troublesome."[15]

As with every religious, his penances consisted in great part in observing the Rule of the Order and obeying the instructions of his superiors. But to these he added other sacrifices, such as the long journeys that he made almost always on foot according to the advice of his Holy Father Dominic, the Dominican *cappa* (cloak) that he often wore even in summer despite the heat, out of solidarity for the brothers in his homeland, who for long periods were forbidden to wear the habit at all. Some of his adventures have a truly picturesque charm, like the time when he set off for a distant railway station through a violent snowstorm and was providentially rescued by a friend of the sisters. Another time, walking to the nuns in Idice, he was caught in a downpour and arrived at his destination soaked. He wanted to start preaching straightway, despite his wet clothes, but he was made to dry himself a little first.[16]

SUNSET

Towards the end of the summer of 1989, Father Týn began to experience the first symptoms of the fatal disease that would quickly lead to his death. At the beginning of November, he was diagnosed with lung cancer that had already metastasized, leaving him only a few months to live.

He suffered intense pains, but endured them with a wonderful strength that he drew from the Crucifix hanging on the wall of his room. He would look towards it and exclaim: "*Fiat voluntas Tua!*" To one close friend, he made this confidence: "Pray for me, because I'm suffering a lot, and I don't want any of it to be lost."

Learning of his son's state of health, his father, Zdenek Týn, asked and obtained permission to take him to

---

15   T. Týn, "Beata Vergine di Lourdes," in R. Schinco, *La Beata sempre Vergine Maria*, 65.

16   Cf. R. Schinco, *La Beata sempre Vergine Maria*, 33.

Germany, "to give his son that material and moral help, and that mutual affection, that the family would for such a short time have the chance to give and receive."[17] Even in his last month of life, and amidst great suffering, Father Tomáš found the strength to celebrate Mass in his room.

He understood that, having received much, he had to give much. He was a theologian and priest whose exceptional gifts had promised him a bright future. But he was called to another and a higher work. Father Tomáš himself, echoing a phrase of his holy father St. Dominic, confided to his confreres that he would be of greater service to the Dominican Order from heaven than on earth.[18] A week before his holy death, when a confrere came to visit him and said with tears: "We must be ready to conform to God's will," Father Tomáš replied with a bright smile: "Let us conform perfectly to God's will."

He died in Neckargemünd on January 1, 1990, just as his homeland was passing peacefully from Communism to democracy: Tomáš' prayers had been answered![19]

The previous evening, the Primate of Prague had presided at a Holy Mass in the cathedral at which a solemn *Te Deum* was sung to give thanks that it was possible once again to practice the faith in public. On the very afternoon of Father Tomáš' death, Holy Mass was televized for the first time in a free Czechoslovakia.[20]

On his tomb, in Neckargemünd in Germany, are inscribed the words of Psalm 42:4: *Et introibo ad altare Dei, ad Deum qui laetificat juventutem meam.*[21] They sum up the profoundly priestly character of his life; a life that ended, like that of Christ, in a total immolation of himself as a victim for the salvation of many.

---

17   *Ibid.* 36.
18   Cf. G. Cavalcoli, O. P., "Tomas Tyn, Un dissidente della ex-Cecoslovacchia."
19   G. Cavalcoli, O. P., "Vita e opere di Tomas Tyn."
20   Cf. R. Schinco, *La Beata sempre Vergine Maria*, 36–37.
21   "I will go in unto the Altar of God, to God, Who giveth joy to my youth."

On October 28, 1989, Father Tomáš had given his last homily in the Basilica of St. Dominic. As he finished speaking by the saint's tomb, he stretched out his arms like the Crucified, and spoke words that are at once a self-portrait and a testament:

> Let us not come to terms with the world! We who have the grace (not the merit) to love the Catholic Church in the purity of tradition, let us allow ourselves to be hated by the world and let us glory in it! It is good to love when you are hated. But not with the uncertain love of false pluralism, but with a love that is as definite as the one, Catholic truth, the truth of Christ crucified, the only Saviour of the world.

TOWARDS GLORY

Immediately after his holy death, Fr Tomáš Týn's friends and admirers in Italy and the Czech Republic, grateful for the benefits received through his ministry, promoted the cause for his beatification. This was officially opened on February 6, 2006 by Cardinal Carlo Caffarra, then Archbishop of Bologna. The decree introducing the cause states:

> Father Tomáš appears as a person firm in the faith, in the midst of the systematic persecution of religion and the temptation to follow the ways of a secularized and Communist humanism. Today his beatification and canonization is desired and requested by numerous people who keep alive the memory of his virtue and that reputation for holiness which was already recognized by so many when he lived among us.[22]

---

22   The bibliography of Father Tomáš Týn's works is available online, at: http://www.studiodomenicano.com/bibliografia.htm

I seek Your Face, Lord!

APOLOGIA FOR THE RELIGIOUS LIFE

RÉGINALD-MARIE RIVOIRE, FSVF

TODAY WE CELEBRATE THE FEAST OF the Presentation of the Lord in the Temple and the Purification of the Blessed Virgin Mary.* Forty days after the birth of Jesus, Mary and Joseph went to the Temple in Jerusalem to present the Child to the Lord as their firstborn and to redeem Him with an offering.

This offering of the Son of God is a model for all those who have dedicated their whole lives to the Lord, for all those who, through the evangelical counsels, have wished to follow our Lord Jesus Christ, the One consecrated to the Father, poor, virginal and obedient.

This mystery of consecration shines throughout the Feast of Candlemas: the consecration of Christ, the consecration of Mary, the consecration of all those who have chosen to follow Jesus Christ for the love of the Kingdom of God. This is eloquently expressed in the Dominican Rite at the time of the Offertory of the Mass, as each brother offers his candle on the altar. February 2nd is the Feast of Religious.

I. Religious life is experiencing an unprecedented crisis in the Church. It seems to be on the verge of sinking, like the boat depicted in the Gospel of this day, taking on water from all sides, and in which our Lord had fallen asleep.

---

* Sermon for the Feast of Candlemas preached in Chémeré-le-Roi, France.

On this real collapse of religious life in the post-conciliar era, the figures speak louder than any words. In 50 years, between 1965 (the end of the Second Vatican Council) and 2015, the number of male religious in the world fell from 330,000 to 200,000; that of sisters and nuns from 1,100,000 to 670,000. In both cases, this represents a decline of almost 40%. And again, these are only global statistics: in Europe and North America, the number dropped by 60%! And the trend is far from reversing. Since 2010, there have been 10,000 fewer sisters each year. This is an unprecedented crisis. Because this almost 50% reduction in the number of religious in the Church is not due to the Black Plague, as in the time of St. Catherine of Siena, but to another plague, the plague of modernism and naturalism. This decline is due to the massive abandonment of religious life and the staggering drop in vocations.

This is a tragic situation that should concern the ecclesiastical authorities far more than it does! Religious life is a manifestation of the holiness of the Church and a constant source of grace. When the heart is wounded, the whole body is sick. With the Sacred Liturgy, religious life, especially the contemplative life, is the place where the virtue of *religion* is exercized at the highest level in the Church. That is why, down through the centuries, the supreme authority has always encouraged religious, has sought to reform them when they have tended to weaken and relax, and has known that it can rely on them to give strength to the whole ecclesial body when needed. Conversely, the decadence of religious life—especially of women—does not bode well for the Church. It is said that "the fish stinks from the head down." Twenty years ago, Cardinal Ratzinger said he was "convinced that the crisis of the Church we are experiencing is largely due to the disintegration of the liturgy." We would like to add: "It is due to the disintegration of the liturgy (during the post-conciliar reform) . . . and of religious life (during the post-conciliar *aggiornamento*)."

Faced with this dramatic observation, what can we do? The answer will obviously depend on whether we are secular or religious.

II. The lay faithful—and the secular clergy—should hold the religious life in high esteem. For this they need to understand it. We do not truly know that which we do not know well. If I believe that "religious" are merely useless beings, cut-price priests, lazy people who have found a "hideout" to avoid tiring themselves out in the parish, I will naturally not be inclined to hold that state in high regard.

If I believe that nuns are just uptight girls who have not found a husband and have had to somehow get hitched at all costs, clearly I will not pray much for female religious vocations and even less encourage this state of life for my pretty daughter who is doing so well with her studies.

Let us remember what religious life is. Religious life, says St. Thomas Aquinas, and the permanent Magisterium after him, is a "state of perfection." This does not mean, of course, that religious are perfect, but that since they are obliged to strive for the perfection of charity—like all Christians—they place themselves in a particular state in order to achieve it, and they equip themselves with highly effective means for this purpose. These means are the three public vows of poverty, chastity and obedience. With these vows, the religious removes all obstacles that might delay or mislead his journey towards the Lord. With these vows, he offers to God, in one go, the whole tree of his life with all its fruits (which is much more meritorious than offering each fruit in turn). And this sacrifice, this self-giving, is a very great act of love for God. "To love is to give everything and to give oneself," said St. Thérèse of Lisieux, and as St. Maximilian Kolbe said, "Love lives and is nourished by sacrifice."

And this sacrifice, which unites us to the offering of our Lord Jesus Christ and His Most Holy Mother, is *an immense grace for the whole Church.* It is fruitful for the salvation of souls. In turn, if they are faithful, it makes of religious a light to enlighten the nations, sons of light, the salt of the earth. Religious bear witness that "the form of this world passes away," that "our city is in the heavens" and that we must "seek things which are above."

This is especially true of nuns, brides of Christ, and even more so of contemplatives. Their radical separation from the world, concretely manifested in their enclosure, is not an escape. By the example of their lives of Christian perfection, by their prayer and penance, they are at the forefront of the struggle of the Church militant. They are the elite, the special forces. St. Teresa of Avila states that they are like the standard-bearer who, in the midst of the battle, is exposed to all the blows and cannot return any of them. They cannot return them, because for the cloistered nun there is no running away, no seeking distractions in apostolic works, no human success—all the things that male religious can experience. Their life is therefore a supernatural life, a life of faith and love.

Religious life belongs to the holiness of the Church. What would the Church be if the consecrated disappeared? Could She still exist?

My dear brothers, cherish religious life, pray for those who pray, pray for female religious vocations. Encourage them.

III. For us other religious, our response to the present crisis of religious life lies in one word: Faithfulness. We solemnly offered ourselves to God on the day of our profession. On that day, through our vows, we gave everything. Everything. *Omnia. Ecce nos relinquimus omnia.* "Now we have given up everything" (Mt. 19:27). Let us never take back what we have given.

There are two ways of being unfaithful. We can, of course, sin directly and gravely against our vows, we can even, God forbid, abandon the religious life. A great number of religious are dispensed from their vows every year. Let us not think that this danger threatens only the progressives. Our treasure rests in earthen vessels: "Whoever flatters himself that he is standing, let him take care not to fall!" (1 Cor. 10:12).

But there is another, more insidious, way to reclaim our gift, to neglect our vocation: to fall asleep, to stand still on the path of holiness. This is the danger of half-heartedness. Nothing is more dangerous for a monastery than a religious who gives up and no longer strives for perfection. He contaminates others, he ruins regular observance.

The small violations of the Rule (particularly the lack of silence, the small accommodations with poverty) pave the way for greater ones. "How serious everything becomes when we stop moving forward" (St. Teresa of Avila), when we stop striving for perfection.

To fight the drowsiness of infidelity, to shake off our torpor, let us remember the "first love" with which Jesus Christ inflamed our hearts: not out of nostalgia, but to nourish that flame. To do this, we must remain with Him in silence and adoration, and awaken in ourselves the will to share His life of poverty, chastity and obedience, and to embrace His Cross.

As symbolized by our procession in the cloister yesterday, religious life is a pilgrimage of the spirit, with its times of marching and its stations; a pilgrimage in search of a Face that sometimes—only rarely—reveals itself, and sometimes—most often—veils itself. *Faciem tuam, Domine, requiram.* "I seek your face, Lord!" (Ps 27:8) May it be the constant desire of our heart, the spring in our step.

May the Blessed Virgin Mary, the Consecrated One *par excellence*, who carried in her arms the very Light, the Word made flesh, guide us on our path through the darkness of this world, to the holy temple of God's glory.

An Ecclesiastical Circumscription for the Older Form of the Latin Rite

LOUIS-MARIE DE BLIGNIÈRES, FSVF*

> All in the Church must preserve unity in essentials. But let all, according to the gifts they have received enjoy a proper freedom, in their various forms of spiritual life and discipline, in their different liturgical rites, and even in their theological elaborations of revealed truth. In all things let charity prevail. If they are true to this course of action, they will be giving ever better expression to the authentic catholicity and apostolicity of the Church.
>
> Second Vatican Council
> *Unitatis redintegratio* 4

CIRCUMSTANCES SEEM TO CALL FOR a fresh look at an old idea: the setting up of an "ecclesiastical circumscription" dedicated to the old Latin rite, especially for the benefit of Catholics living in French dioceses. As we shall see, there is nothing revolutionary about this proposal. After outlining the reasons for which such a reflection is opportune today, we shall briefly review the proposals that have been made in this regard in recent decades. We shall then outline our proposed legal solution and discuss its advantages.

---

* Fr. Louis-Marie de Blignières, the founder of the Fraternity of St. Vincent Ferrer, is the author of several works of spirituality, theology, and metaphysics. [This article was translated by John Pepino, PhD.]

I. THE PRESENT SITUATION

The publication of the motu proprio *Traditionis custodes* on July 16, 2021, and that of the documents of the Congregation for Divine Worship in December 2021, have opened up a period of doubt and uncertainty among those Catholics who are both faithful to hierarchical communion and also, to quote St. John Paul II, attached to the "previous ... forms of the Latin tradition."[1] Questions that had found a peaceful solution (or at least an acceptable status quo) in 2007 with the motu proprio *Summorum pontificum* reappeared in sharper focus. The apostolate of the institutes that had been erected after the motu proprio *Ecclesia Dei* of July 2, 1988 became difficult.

Fortunately, the decree granted by the Holy Father to the Priestly Fraternity of St. Peter on February 11, 2022 provided a renewed guarantee that the liturgical books mentioned in the decrees of erection would continue to be used in the houses of those institutes. A number of diocesan ordinaries also manifested the "greater solicitude and paternity towards people" to which Pope Francis had invited the bishops in the October 27, 2022 message from the Cardinal Secretary of State at the opening of the Plenary Assembly of the Bishops of France in Lourdes.

Yet the work of these institutes, some of which are by nature dedicated to the apostolic life, is severely restricted by a number of bishops. Some apply to the letter the indications of *Traditionis custodes* and its accompanying Letter, as well as the directives of the [now] Dicastery for Divine Worship; sometimes they even go beyond them. These restrictions or prohibitions mainly concern sacramental ministry (baptisms, confirmations, marriages, funerals, and even faculties to hear confessions) and in a few cases, catechesis.

---

1   John Paul II, motu proprio *Ecclesia Dei adflicta*, July 2, 1988, in *AAS*, 80 (1988), 1495-1498.

This has led to a paradoxical situation. Since 1988, the Society of St. Pius X has acted outside of any hierarchical mandate. Yet since the faculties granted to it by Pope Francis in 2015 and 2017 (a cause of joy for the good of the faithful), in certain respects (notably marriages according to the old ritual) it enjoys greater favor than do traditional institutes in full communion with the Holy See.[2]

This situation, which follows fourteen years of relative peace (2007–2021), is shocking to many lay faithful and priests of various ecclesial horizons well beyond "traditional Catholics." This is particularly the case since, in many dioceses, recent "synodal approaches" had invited the Catholic faithful to show good will towards all. The Church is short of priests and is facing major difficulties in the areas of faith and morals, both externally and internally. How, then, are we to understand the obstacles placed in the way of the apostolate of priests whose pastoral zeal the faithful have witnessed, particularly during the lockdowns, and whose catechetical effectiveness and dedication to works of formation and evangelization they so appreciate? The orthodoxy of these priests is never in question. Their obedience is manifest in their ministries, which they exercise on a mission they have received from legitimate pastors. Their sense of the Church is reflected in their insistence on meeting, whatever the cost, the high demands of hierarchical communion, as opposed to the easier path available outside it....

Unfortunately, the situation seems to have reached an impasse.

---

2   Pope Francis, *Letter According to Which an Indulgence Is Granted to the Faithful on the Occasion of the Extraordinary Jubilee of Mercy*, September 1, 2015, in *AAS*, 107 (2015), 974–976. The faithful who confess their sins to priests of the SSPX during the Year of Mercy (December 8, 2015–November 12, 2016) "shall validly and licitly receive the absolution of their sins." At the end of that year, the measure was extended *sine die* in the Apostolic Letter *Misericordia et misera*, November 21, 2016, in *AAS*, 108 (2016), 1311–1327. —Letter of the president of the Pontifical Commission Ecclesia Dei to the episcopal conferences, March 27, 2017, in AAS, 109 (2017), 426–427.

I here propose to reflect on a possible solution: an ecclesiastical circumscription dedicated to the old Latin rite. It would concern Catholics attached to earlier forms of the Latin tradition who reside in French dioceses. France has been the historical heartland of the traditionalist question, and its specific situation is the one I know best.[3] This dedicated circumscription would have various advantages for priests and faithful alike, and could relieve pastors of a responsibility that can be difficult to shoulder. It would also contribute in its own way to the "ecumenical credibility" of the Church herself,[4] in keeping with the final indications of the *Pastoral Constitution on the Church in the Modern World*:

> Such a mission requires in the first place that we foster within the Church herself mutual esteem, reverence and harmony, through the full recognition of lawful diversity. Thus all those who compose the one People of God, both pastors and the general faithful, can engage in dialogue with ever abounding fruitfulness. For the bonds which unite the faithful are mightier than anything dividing them. Hence, let there be *unity in what is necessary, freedom in what is unsettled, and charity in any case.*[5]

As Cardinal Ratzinger pointed out to me in 1990, a "capacity for internal reconciliation" is a "test of ecumenical sincerity."

---

3   It is for others to study whether such a dedicated circumscription would be opportune in other regions of the Catholic world.
4   The president of the Department for Exterior Relations of the Patriarchate of Moscow, Cyril of Smolensk (later patriarch of Moscow) publicly expressed his joy in 2007 at the publication of *Summorum pontificum.*
5   Concilium Vaticanum II, *Gaudium et spes*, 92, December 7, 1965, in *AAS*, 58 (1966), 1025–1115. The saying at the end of this text is drawn from St. John XXIII's encyclical *Ad Petri cathedram*, June 29, 1959, in *AAS*, 51 (1959), 497–511; St. John XXIII indicates (n. 72) that "this saying has been expressed in various ways and attributed to various authors."

II. THE DEVELOPMENT OF THE IDEA OF
A DEDICATED ECCLESIASTICAL CIRCUMSCRIPTION

Since 1988, the desirability of a dedicated ecclesiastical circumscription for the old Latin rite has been raised on several occasions by members of what has sometimes been called the "Ecclesia Dei movement," i.e., "traditionalists" committed to full communion with the Holy See and the Catholic hierarchy.

Let us begin with an anecdote that is significant for our purposes. It will allow us to date the beginning of the discernment process mentioned in the subtitle of this section. During a stay in Rome from June 9 to 16, 1988, specifically devoted to research in the archives of the Congregation for the Doctrine of the Faith, Father de Saint Laumer and I passed a note to Cardinal Ratzinger. It contained certain suggestions concerning the situation created by Archbishop Marcel Lefebvre's recent announcement that he would consecrate bishops without a papal mandate. The note suggested the rapid announcement by the Holy See of measures to support the traditionalist faithful who would not follow Archbishop Lefebvre, and raised the possibility of the episcopal consecration of a priest from within this movement, for the pastoral care of these faithful. The cardinal met us in a corridor and said: "Was it you who gave me the note? Thank you, it's in line with some of the current thinking."

July 1988: A request for a bishop

In Rome on July 6, the priests who had left the Priestly Society of St. Pius X and I drew up a "Resumption of the Protocol of Agreement" in light of the motu proprio *Ecclesia Dei*" (*Reprise du Protocole d'accord à la lumière du motu proprio* Ecclesia Dei). Based on the Protocol signed on May 5, 1988 by Cardinal Ratzinger and Archbishop Lefebvre,[6] the aim was to present concrete proposals to

6   https://www.fssp.org/en/protocol-between-the-holy-see-and-the-priestly-society-of-st-pius-x/ [accessed 21 February 2024—*trans.*].

the Holy See for traditionalists who wished to remain in communion with the hierarchy, while preserving the "traditional pedagogies of the faith"[7] and Latin rites that predate the reform. Specifically, the text contemplates, "in view of the particular situations mentioned, *the ordination of a bishop drawn from these very groups*" (3.2); it goes on to say, "[i]n view of the diversity of the organizations at work and the complexity of the problems raised, we suggest the study of the creation of *a personal diocese under the authority of a bishop*" (4.2).

On July 15 of the same year, a larger meeting took place at the Benedictine abbey of Fontgombault, chaired by Mgr. Camille Perl, Secretary of the Pontifical Commission *Ecclesia Dei*, and including, in addition to the priests already mentioned, priests from *Opus sacerdotale*, the founders of *Opus Mariæ* (which would later become the Canons Regular of the Mother of God Lagrasse) and the Italian priests who were later to found *Opus Mariæ Matris Ecclesiæ*. The second point mentioned (4.2) was reformulated: "For practical and psychological reasons, which the recent dissidence has made critical, the Holy See commits to giving to *this family of like-minded Catholics one or more bishops of its own as soon as possible*, according to a juridical formula to be determined."

This "Resumption of the Protocol of Agreement," signed by twenty-four priests, was given to Mgr. Perl to pass on to Cardinal Paul-Augustin Mayer, President of the Pontifical Commission *Ecclesia Dei*.

7　This expression is that found in the "Entreaty for Peace" (*Supplique pour la paix*) signed by 65 priests and lay personalities and submitted to Cardinal Ratzinger on March 22, 1988. This text mentions the "eminently pastoral concern" for the old Latin rite, "a form in which so many souls' faith in the Eucharistic Mystery finds its nourishment and expression." It also mentions the "disciplines of prayer and spirituality" of those faithful, as well as the "great spiritual fruits that have already been reaped through the traditional pedagogies of the faith." [Father de Blignières uses the term "traditional pedagogies" so as to encompass not only the older liturgy, but also the associated discipline, catechism, and devotional practices—*Editor's note*.].

September 1990: Dom Gérard proposes the creation of Vicariates

Dom Gérard Calvet, Abbot of Le Barroux, accompanied by some of his monks, met Pope John Paul II in private audience. He raised the possibility of creating apostolic vicariates dedicated to the old Latin rite.

Finally, in the last part of his speech, which was delivered but not published "out of discretion," Dom Gérard proposed a "solution" to resolve the difficulties encountered by communities, priests, and faithful attached to the traditional liturgy: the creation of an apostolic vicariate that would make them independent from the dioceses....

The idea of instituting an apostolic vicariate or ordinariate specifically for the faithful attached to traditional rites was not unique to Dom Gérard and his prior, Father Anselme, who took a keen interest in institutional and canonical issues. But Le Barroux Abbey was the first to suggest such a solution to the Holy See. This kind of structure already existed in various forms: the ordinariate for the armed forces or ordinariates for the faithful of the Eastern rites. This solution would be used under the next pontificate for the Anglican clergy and faithful who wished to return to Catholic communion.[8] The idea was taken up again at meetings with Cardinal Ratzinger.[9]

May–June 1991: A petition from the United States of America

Éric de Saventhem, president and founder of the International Federation *Una Voca*, in an article titled "For an Apostolic Vicariate," published in *Una Voce* (May–June 1991), wrote:

---

8 Benedict XVI, Apostolic Constitution *Anglicanorum coetibus*, November 4, 2009, in *AAS*, 101 (2009), 985–990; Congregation for the Doctrine of the Faith, general executory decree issuing complementary norms for the apostolic constitution *Anglicanorum coetibus Norme Complementari*, 4 November 2009, https://www.vatican.va/roman_curia/congregations/cfaith/documents/rc_con_cfaith_doc_20091104_norme-anglicanorum-coetibus_en.html (9 March 2022) (2009); id., general decree *Each Ordinariate*, March 19, 2019, in *AAS*, 111 (2019), 749–756.
9 Yves Chiron, *Histoire des traditionalistes* (Paris: Tallendier, 2022), 369–371 [English version forthcoming at Angelico press—*trans.*].

As many of you know, our sister association in the USA has launched a popular petition in favour of the erection of "traditional ordinariates." The aim is to create canonical structures that are independent of existing diocesan bureaucracies, enabling the peaceful development of communities of the faithful whose spiritual life is nourished by the rites in force until 1962. By way of analogy, the petition refers to military ordinariates, created according to the norms of the apostolic constitution *Spirituali militum curæ* of April 21, 1986.[10] These ordinariates are "juridically likened to dioceses" and constitute "particular ecclesiastical circumscriptions."[11] Military ordinaries, normally invested with episcopal dignity, enjoy "all the rights of diocesan bishops" (II). Their jurisdiction is "personal," so that it "is exercised over those who belong to the ordinariate"; it is "ordinary" in both the internal and external forum; and it is "proper but cumulative with the jurisdiction of the diocesan bishop," since those belonging to the ordinariate continue to be faithful "of that diocesan Church to whose people they belong by reason of domicile or rite" (IV).

Based on this analogy, the American petition calls for—and I quote: "the erection of a traditional ordinariate which, like the military ordinariate in the United States, would have the status of a national diocese. It would provide for the pastoral needs of traditional Catholics under the direction of a bishop appointed specifically

---

10   John Paul II, Apostolic Constitution *Spirituali militum curae* [*SMC*], April 21, 1986, in *AAS*, 78 (1986), 481–486.

11   *SMC*, I, Par. 1. "The Military Ordinariates, which may also be called Army Ordinariates, and are juridically comparable to diocese, are special ecclesiastical territories, governed by proper statutes issued by the Apostolic See, in which will be determined in greater detail the prescriptions of the present constitution; agreements between the Holy See and various States are, where they exist, still valid. (Cfr. *Codex Iuris Canonici*, can. 3)." [Note that *circumscriptio ecclesiastica* is translated as "ecclesiastical territory"—*trans.*].

for this task by the Holy Father. With the support of this bishop, parishes and schools could
be established, free from control and interference
by the diocesan bureaucracies, so often hostile
to our legitimate aspirations. If God inspires
vocations among our young people, there could
also be 'traditional' seminaries and new religious
communities. All of them—parishes, schools,
seminaries and houses of religious—would be
linked directly to Rome through the traditional
ordinariate, and its bishop."[12]

1993–1994

Also in 1993, the Traditional Mass Society (TMS), the
American branch of *Una Voce*, gathered signatures in the
USA calling for freedom to celebrate the traditional Mass
and for the creation of a "Traditional Apostolic Vicariate
covering the USA and Canada" to unite, organize, and
protect. Some 40,000 signatures were gathered. TMS President William R. Opelle was able to present the petition
to John Paul II during an audience on February 28, 1994.
In the accompanying letter, he wrote: "The signatories
(who include hardly any so-called "Lefebvrists," since the
priests of the Society of St. Pius X told their people not
to sign) represent but a minute fraction of those U. S. and
Canadian Catholics who want to live and pray according
to the Church's tradition."[13]

On September 27, 1994, Éric de Saventhem sent a letter
to Archbishop Re, Substitue for the Secretary of State, to
remind him that the request had yet to receive an answer:

> ... Our North American friends have been wait-
> ing seven months to hear what action will be
> taken in response to this petition. And since its

12   Éric de Saventhem, "Pour un Vicariat apostolique," *Una Voce*
(May–June 1991).
13   Letter (dated January 31, 1994) printed in *The Latin Mass* Magazine (May–June 1994) and reprinted in the UNA VOCE/USA-Tradi-
tional Mass Society Newsletter, Summer 1995 [Copy kindly provided
by Byron Smith, Secretary, *Una Voce America*—trans.].

purpose is "to obtain a measure of exemption from the dictates of the all-powerful diocesan and national bureaucracies," the signatories won't be satisfied with a simple acknowledgement of receipt from Your Excellency, informing them that "*per competentiam*," their petition has been forwarded to the President of the U.S. Bishops' Conference!

June 2001: An official request from Ecclesia Dei communities

On June 4, 2001, a *Plea to the Holy Father* was presented in Chartres to Cardinal Castrillon Hoyos, President of the Pontifical Commission *Ecclesia Dei*.[14] It was signed by almost all community superiors and lay personalities in the *Ecclesia Dei* movement.[15] This plea included the following request:

> As a solution to some very painful exclusions, we suggest that Your Holiness confer on the Pontifical Commission *Ecclesia Dei* (cf. canon 372 § 2) the power to institute "Apostolic Vicariates," so that the communities depending on them may enjoy a broad exemption, enabling them to establish themselves and exercise their proper ends within the dioceses. Without a hierarchical body of this sort, the establishment, growth, and sometimes survival of our communities are compromised today, for lack of simply being able to exist or to welcome the many vocations that present themselves.

---

14   On April 26, 2001, I wrote to Fr. Joseph Bisig, one of the founders of the Fraternity of St. Peter: "The development of the situation over the last twelve years (especially the outlook among the bishops of Germany and France) indicates that an Ordinariate, a Prelature, or a Ritual Church is the most coherent and practicable solution, despite the limitations we had clearly perceived at several meetings in the early years of *Ecclesia Dei*." The June 4th plea was presented by Fr. Bisig to Cardinal Josef Ratzinger, who showed himself favorable to this solution.

15   The Institute of the Dominican Sisters of the Holy Ghost (Pontcallec) and the *Action Familiale et Scolaire* (Arnaud de Lassus) did not sign it.

July 2001: The Holy See considers this solution for the SSPX

The Holy See itself devised the solution of a dedicated ecclesiastical circumscription. The structure of an apostolic administration was proposed to the Society of St. Pius X. Bishop Bernard Fellay, then Superior General of the SSPX, remarked:

> An apostolic administration is better than a personal prelature. First of all, a personal prelature is not necessarily governed by a bishop. An apostolic administration, which is a quasi-diocese, usually is. Secondly and most importantly, the action of an apostolic administration is not limited to its members. *Opus Dei*, which is the personal prelature in existence today, is not subject to the local bishop in everything that concerns its members, but it cannot consider any external action without the bishop's agreement. With an apostolic administration, we would escape this restriction. We would have been in a position to carry out an autonomous apostolic action without having to ask the diocesan bishop for authorization, since we would have a real diocese, with the particularity of extending to the whole globe. It's very important that such a proposal was made, because after all, such a juridical solution is unprecedented, it's *sui generis*. [16]

There is an interesting precedent here. This possibility might easily be offered to Catholics who are subject to the Holy See and who request it, since it has been proposed to a group that acts outside the hierarchical mission and did not request it.

January–March 2002: A circumscription for the old rite is created in Campos, Brazil

In a decree dated January 18, 2002, the Congregation for Bishops erected the personal Apostolic Administration of "St. John Mary Vianney" in the diocese of Campos (Brazil),

---

16   *Pacte* 56 (July 2001).

where a large proportion of the clergy and faithful had remained attached to the traditional liturgy. Paragraph III reads as follows:

> To the Apostolic Administration is assigned the faculty of celebrating the Holy Eucharist, the other sacraments, the Liturgy of the Hours, and other liturgical actions according to the Roman Rite and liturgical discipline prescribed by St. Pius V, with the modifications introduced by his successors down to Blessed John XXIII.

On March 19, 2002 I wrote to express my gratitude to Cardinal Castrillon Hoyos, who was responsible for making this erection possible. In that letter I noted:

> A Personal Apostolic Administration with cumulative jurisdiction, while safeguarding communion with the local Church, actualizes in the case of Campos the promise made in 1988 to the "traditionalist" faithful by the Holy See, which "assured them that all measures would be taken to guarantee their identity in full communion with the Catholic Church." [17]

2002-2006: The Holy See contemplates an Ordinariate for all traditionalists

For some years, the leadership of the *Ecclesia Dei* Commission, Cardinal Castrillon Hoyos and Mgr. Camille Perl, were interested in developing a similar formula for traditionalists in general. "Mgr Perl is in favour of the idea of such a personal apostolic administration open to all the 'Traddies' of the world," Fr. Bisig wrote to me March 13, 2002. The dicasteries concerned were giving serious consideration to the project. In May 2003, informed sources estimated that it had already been drafted, and would probably be announced at the Mass celebrated by Cardinal Castrillon Hoyos on May 24, 2003 at Santa Maria Maggiore.

---

17   Information Note from the Holy See, June 18, 1988, *La Documentation Catholique* 1966, 739.

In an interview with Dr. Ralf Siebenburger and the *Una Voce* International leadership on March 13, 2004, Cardinal Castrillon Hoyos "repeated that he had abandoned any idea of giving us our own jurisdiction."[18] The cardinal declared that the erection of the Campos personal administration was a very special case. He repeated this on May 5, 2004 in an interview with the *Latin Mass* magazine. Moreover, according to what Archbishop Perl told Dr. Siebenburger, the Roman authorities "feared protests from the bishops and episcopal conferences."

Yet, the possibility of personal apostolic administrations was still being discussed in the Holy See in the early days of Benedict XVI's pontificate. In a report of a visit to Rome with Father de Saint Laumer in February 2006, I wrote the following:

> Various projects are under study to support groups attached to traditional pedagogies *(Ecclesia Dei* groups and the like). There is talk of creating one or more personal apostolic administrations endowed with specific jurisdiction. These projects are being pushed by Cardinal Hoyos and Fr. Guimarães, CSSR, of the Congregation for the Clergy (the curial official responsible for Campos), but at present seem to be of a more "prospective" nature. Opposition from the bishops' conferences is feared, and Rome is seeking ways to disarm it. Hopefully, things will become clearer around Easter.[19]

The last initiative of this sort for this period was taken in October 2006 by Father John Berg, Superior General of the FSSP, and myself. In a joint letter to Cardinal Castrillon Hoyos, we mentioned three possibilities for overcoming "persistent reticence and opposition." One of these was as follows: "Couldn't we set up an Apostolic Administration for France, on the model of that of Campos in Brazil, or

---

18   As reported at www.dici.org/actualite (May 1, 2004).
19   "Report on the trip to Rome, February 8–18, 2006," dated February 22, 2006.

an Ordinariate with cumulative jurisdiction, as there is for the armed forces in various countries?"[20]

2006–2022: *The Holy See tries a different path with Summorum pontificum*

The prospect of creating ecclesiastical circumscriptions dedicated to the old Latin rite was finally put on hold after 2006. At the time, Cardinal Castrillon Hoyos was mainly concerned with overtures towards the SSPX. In July 2007, with *Summorum pontificum*, Benedict XVI tried a completely different path.

Pope Francis, from 2013 to the publication of the motu proprio *Traditionis custodes* in 2021, left the issue as he had received it from his predecessor.

March–June 2022: New proposals since Traditionis Custodes

I wrote the following in an article published in *Sedes Sapientiæ* 159 (March 2022):

> Here is a positive suggestion to conclude these reflections. If the "Ordinary Form" vs "Extraordinary Form" distinction is confusing, why not think of another distinction, and distinguish not two forms, but two Latin rites in their own right, the "old" rite and the "modern" rite? This could lead to the creation of personal ecclesiastical circumscriptions with the right to celebrate all liturgical actions according to the 1962 Roman Rite.[21] The old Roman rite, venerable by virtue of its antiquity, would thus be respected, just as St. Pius V had respected venerable rites other than the Roman rite.
>
> Wouldn't granting to the traditional Roman Mass the status of a particular rite with its own

---

20 Information Note and Plea to Cardinal Castrillon Hoyos, President of the *Ecclesia Dei* Pontifical Commission, October 7, 2006.
21 The groups of faithful joining such hierarchical communities would belong to the Latin Church. As such, they would remain subject to the Code of Canon Law, except for the special discipline enjoyed by their hierarchical community [footnote in the original].

ecclesiastical circumscriptions (prelature, ordinariate, apostolic administration), as we have repeatedly proposed to the Holy See,[22] be an elegant solution that respects the rights of all?

Father Réginald-Marie Rivoire, in a work entitled *Does Traditionis Custodes Pass the Juridical Rationality Test?*,[23] made the following proposal:

What, then, will be the future of *TC*? The history of canon law, even in recent times, does not lack examples of laws that quickly fell into disuse because they were not adequate to the social reality they were intended to order.[24] However, the posterity of this motu proprio could well be unexpected. Insofar as it seems to ratify the abandonment of the vocabulary of "two forms of the Roman Rite," it could paradoxically constitute an important step towards the canonical recognition of two Latin rites in their own right, namely the "Roman" rite and the "modern" rite. Should this reality, albeit totally unprecedented, be fully taken into account by the legislator, and given the fact that "all legitimately recognized rites are equal in right and dignity" (cf. *SC* 4), the logical consequence would be the erection of personal ecclesiastical circumscriptions enjoying the faculty of celebrating all liturgical actions according to the traditional Roman Rite.[25]

---

22   E.g., in the May 7, 2001 "Plea to the Holy Father" signed by twenty superiors of traditional communities and twenty lay movement leaders; cf. Chiron, *Traditionalistes*, 388 [footnote in the original].
23   Réginald-Marie Rivoire, *Does* Traditionis Custodes *Pass the Juridical Rationality Test?* William Barker trans. (Lincoln, NE: Os Justi Press, 2022), 82–83.
24   The most emblematic example of such non-acceptance—a true textbook example—is that of the Apostolic Constitution *Veterum Sapientia* of February 22, 1962, signed with great solemnity by John XXIII on the very altar of St. Peter's Confession, and which intended to promote the study and use of Latin in the Church [footnote in the original].
25   Fr. Donneaud considers the at least theoretical possibility of this, even if he finds it difficult to imagine (cf. H. Donneaud, "Le pape François, garant de la doctrine liturgique de saint Pie V," 50n19 [footnote in the original].

To summarize this historical overview: a legal proposal went through a progressive formalization and became the object of increasingly pressing and universal demands.

III. A POSSIBLE SOLUTION: A DEDICATED ECCLESIASTICAL CIRCUMSCRIPTION

A group made up of lay faithful and priests

The key issue in discussing a dedicated ecclesiastical circumscription for the old Latin rite is whether this rite corresponds to a legitimate and sufficiently differentiated ecclesial reality within the universal Church. Do the lay faithful and priests with a firm attachment to the old Latin Rite and the "traditional pedagogies of the faith,"[26] and who are in communion with the Holy See and the rest of the Church, form a sufficiently specific group for the solution of a dedicated ecclesiastical circumscription to be opportune?

In my view, the answer is undeniably yes. According to the Holy See, the characteristics of this group of the faithful amount to a genuine "identity" which it is legitimate to guarantee.[27] In his motu proprio *Ecclesia Dei*, Pope John Paul II gave precise indications about the components of this identity. The liturgy is mentioned three times (5c, 6a, and 6c). This is not, however, the only salient feature the Pope highlights in describing the identity of the "Catholic faithful who feel attached to some previous ... forms of the Latin tradition." Significantly, *spirituality* and *the apostolate* are mentioned first, spirituality occurring twice (5a and 6a) and the apostolate once (5a). The Pope also mentions *discipline* (5c). Here are the relevant passages:

> However, it is necessary that all the Pastors and the other faithful have a new awareness, not only of the lawfulness but also of the treasure

---

26 See n. 7 above.

27 On June 18, 1988, the Information Note mentioned above assured these Catholics that "every measure would be taken to *guarantee their identity* within the full communion of the Church."

for the Church of a diversity of charisms, traditions of *spirituality* and *apostolate*, which also
constitutes the beauty of unity in variety: of that
blended "harmony" which the earthly Church
raises up to Heaven under the impulse of the
Holy Spirit (5a).[28]

To all those Catholic faithful who feel attached
to some previous *liturgical* and *disciplinary* forms
of the Latin tradition I wish to manifest my will
to facilitate their ecclesial communion by means
of the necessary measures to guarantee respect
for their rightful aspirations. In this matter I
ask for the support of the bishops and of all
those engaged in the pastoral ministry in the
Church (5c).

[A] Commission is instituted whose task it
will be to collaborate with the bishops, with the
Departments of the Roman Curia and with the
circles concerned, for the purpose of facilitating
full ecclesial communion of priests, seminarians, religious communities or individuals until
now linked in various ways to the Fraternity
founded by Archbishop Lefebvre, who may wish
to remain united to the Successor of Peter in the
Catholic Church, while preserving their *spiritual*
and *liturgical* traditions, in the light (*juxta*) of
the Protocol signed on 5 May last by Cardinal
Ratzinger and Archbishop Lefebvre (6a).

[M]oreover, respect must everywhere be shown
for the feelings of all those who are attached
to the Latin *liturgical* tradition, by a wide and
generous application of the directives already
issued some time ago by the Apostolic See for
the use of the Roman Missal according to the
typical edition of 1962 (6c).

This description applies to a group of the faithful
that is both consistent and distinct enough from other

---

28   I am here using a more literal translation than the official one;
see John Pepino, "*Ex Oriente lux*: St. John Paul II, the Eastern Rites,
and the Traditional Roman Rite," *Sedes Sapientiæ* Special English-
Language Issue (2022), 94.

groups—while remaining within Catholic unity—that the Holy Father, in speaking of it, used the *same vocabulary one can use to speak of the ritual Churches.* We shall return to this.

This group manifests a consistency beyond the merely liturgical

It is now widely recognized that the history of the contemporary Church has been marked by abuses and controversies affecting catechesis, the understanding of Scripture, the doctrinal continuity of the magisterium, apostolic methods, and spirituality. The documentation is abundant.[29] It is significant that St. John Paul II, in *Ecclesia Dei,* refers not only to the four notes mentioned above, but also to "erroneous interpretations and arbitrary and abusive applications *in matters of doctrine.*"

Half a century on, bishops, priests, and laymen who are in communion with the Catholic Church and who accept the substantial doctrinal continuity this implies can agree that considerable mutations affecting the practice of the Catholic religion took place during this period, some of them undermining faith and morals. As a result, a certain number of the faithful have kept to the "traditional pedagogies of the faith" while adhering to the

---

29   To mention only a few relatively recent works: Jean-Miguel Garrigues, *Par des sentiers resserrés. Itinéraires d'un religieux dans des temps incertains* (Paris: Presses de la Renaissance, 2007); Yann Raison du Cleuziou, *De la contemplation à la contestation. La politisation des dominicains de la Province de France (années 1940–1970)* (Paris: Belin, 2016); Guillaume Cuchet, *Comment notre monde a cessé d'être chrétien. Anatomie d'un effondrement* (Paris, Seuil, 2018) [English summary and review in *Catholic World Report* (September 13, 2022)—*trans.*]; Yves Chiron, *Histoire des traditionalistes* (Paris, Éditions Tallandier, 2021) [English version forthcoming at Angelico Press—*trans.*]; Yvon Tranvouez, *L'ivresse et le vertige. Vatican II, le moment 68 et la crise catholique (1960–1980)* (Paris: Desclée de Brouwer, 2021); Sr Ambroise-Dominique Salleron, *Louis Salleron. Au service du bien commun* (Versailles: Via Romana, 2022). [For the UK and the USA, see Hugh McLeod, *The Religious Crisis of the 1960s* (Oxford: Oxford University Press, 2007); Callum G. Brown, *The Death of Christian Britain. Understanding Secularisation, 1800-2000* (Oxford: Routledge, 2009); Stephen Bullivant, *Mass Exodus: Catholic Disaffiliation in Britain and America Since Vatican II* (Oxford: Oxford University Press, 2019)—*trans.*]

magisterium and respecting hierarchical communion.

The *culture* (to use the word) in which these priests, religious, and laymen are formed, and within which they experience pastoral ministry, is a *culture of roots*. They "[t]ake care of the roots, because from the roots comes the strength that will make [one] grow, prosper and bear fruit."[30] In the words of the Lord, we need soil, good soil, to take in the seed (cf. Lk. 8:5–15). It's also a *culture of inventiveness*, for when it comes to pastoral formulas, they are able to find forms of communication best suited to today; and in the fields of theology, philosophy, and science, they can push ahead with at times novel studies.[31] For them, "identity and dialogue are not enemies."[32] All in all, this culture represents a richness for the Church.

The group we are here talking about has repeatedly shown that it is firmly attached to 1) its traditional practices, which it is not about to abandon, 2) effective communion with the Church hierarchy. It therefore seems both legitimate and opportune to give these faithful their rightful place in the Church.

An overview of the history of the Church over the last few decades reveals various versions of a practical proposal of the type I am here suggesting. As early as 1976, Archbishop Marcel Lefebvre asked to be allowed to "perform the experiment of Tradition."[33] This expression

---

30   Pope Francis, Video-message to indigenous youth, Panama, January 18, 2019.

31   The following are contributions from the Fraternity of St. Vincent Ferrer: in biblical theology, an original reading of the cycles of filiation (A.-M. Crignon, *Qui es-tu mon fils ?* [Paris: Cerf, 2019]); in ecclesiology, the innovative exploration of the authentic Magisterium (A.-M. Aubry, *Obéir ou assentir* [Paris: Desclée de Brouwer, 2015]); in metaphysics, a deepening of Thomism that integrates modern intuitions (L.-M. de Blignières, *Le mystère de l'être* [Paris: Vrin, 2007]); in science, a "Thomistic look at evolution" (*Sedes Sapientiæ* 106 and 164)....

32   Pope Francis, Post-Synodal Apostolic Exhortation *Querida Amazonia*, 2 February 2020, 37.

33   This "experiment with Tradition" started out as a slogan, then

must be understood in a broad sense. What is meant here is not Tradition directly, in the theological sense of a transmission of the revealed deposit (the Church necessarily experiences this, as it is part of its very substance), but the practice of traditional pedagogies of the faith, which remain tried and true, even in modern times.

This is also the thinking behind Father Louis Bouyer's common-sense proposal for a solution. It is worth noting that his proposal for freedom for the old Mass, far from giving rise to quarrels, would be a source of peace.

> Certainly local authorities and even, it has to be said, the Roman authorities, seem to tolerate even the most extreme forms of deviation, not only from the general tradition, but very precisely even from the new Missal. They do condemn only one thing absolutely, however: the old Missal, which after all has been used for centuries.... I'm going to say something very simple here: if the Paul VI missal had been introduced, while allowing the Pius V missal to be kept where desired for an interim period that could have lasted as long as necessary, things would have gone very smoothly, without violence, and the transition would have been easy. Paul VI's missal would undoubtedly have caught on, and certain modifications could have been made to take account

---

became a project. The expression first appeared in a talk Archbishop Lefebvre gave at the Mutualité Lecture Hall in April 1973. With some wit, the prelate said regarding the Mass of St. Pius V: "I follow the directives given for group Masses (laughter). I am asking to perform an experiment with Tradition (applause)"; Bernard Tissier de Mallerais, *Marcel Lefebvre*, 475, quoting *Rivarol* (5 April 1973). He reprised the expression, with greater pathos, at the "Mass in Lille" (June 29, 1976): "[T]hat is what I will ask the Holy Father if he wishes to receive me: 'Most Holy Father, let us carry out this experiment of Tradition,'" ibid., 490. Indeed, on September 11, 1976, during the audience that Paul VI had granted him at Castel Gandolfo, Archbishop Lefebvre said to him: "Most Holy Father.... Let me carry out this experiment of Tradition. Let there be, amid all the experiments of this time, the experiment of what has been done for twenty centuries." [This last sentence is not in the English version of Tissier de Mallerais, *Marcel Lefebvre—trans.*].

of certain criticisms. It would have been quite
normal to allow those who so wished to keep
the old missal, while introducing the new one.[34]

*This group of faithful presents characteristics analogous to those
that make the creation of ecclesiastical circumscriptions
opportune*

1. Let us start with the central issue: the liturgy. Does
the celebration of the sacraments according to the rites
prior to the post-conciliar reforms have characteristics
comparable to those of the Eastern rites?

From a phenomenological point of view, this seems
certain. Anyone entering an Eastern Rite church in the
early 1970s—I am here speaking from personal experience—would have been gripped by an atmosphere of
sacrality, sadly absent from almost all celebrations according to the Latin Rite promulgated by St. Paul VI. Admittedly, the tone was unmistakably distinct from that of
the old Latin rite. But the organization of the sacred
space, the wall decorations, the orientation of the celebrant, the use of a sacred language, the beauty of the
ministers' vestments, the use of incense, the choreography,
the secrecy of some of the celebrant's prayers (notably
the anaphora, which had to be followed in a booklet,
just as a Latin Catholic follows the canon of the Mass
of St. Pius V), the sacrificial emphasis of many of the
orations ... all this made the Latin layman, exiled as he
was from his own liturgy, find himself immediately in
familiar territory, so to speak.

This impression has an undeniable liturgical and theological basis. It was notably formulated by St. John Paul II:

> St. John Paul II expressed himself on the tradi-
> tional Roman liturgy on a few occasions.... A

---

34   L. Bouyer, *Le Métier de théologien* (Paris: Ad Solem, 1978; 2nd
ed., 2005), 85–87. This solution as proposed is temporary, but with a
broad application: "an interim period that could have lasted *as long
as necessary.*" This seems to imply: "as long as there shall be faithful
attached to the older forms."

comparison of these texts with the same pope's interventions on the Oriental Rites and the Vatican II documents that inform them, indicates that the *Polish pope viewed the traditional Roman liturgy just as he did the Oriental rites* in relation to the then recently promulgated liturgy, namely: as a treasure that is part of the diverse liturgical patrimony of the Church rather than a threat to its unity, well-suited to express the mysteries it contains, and worthy of both protection on the part of the hierarchy and encouragement in its fidelity to itself.[35]

This startling joint praise of the Eastern rites and the old Latin rite goes quite far, since it concerns the very substance of the liturgy:

The People of God need to see priests and deacons behave in a way that is full of reverence and dignity, in order to help them to penetrate invisible things without unnecessary words or explanations. In the Roman Missal of Saint Pius V, as in several Eastern liturgies, there are very beautiful prayers through which the priest expresses the most profound sense of humility and reverence before the Sacred Mysteries: they reveal the very substance of the Liturgy.[36]

It would seem, therefore, that if only from a strictly liturgical point of view, there is a serious basis for the constitution of the old Latin rite, if not as a ritual church, at least as a specific ecclesiastical circumscription.

2. This opinion is reinforced by the fact that priests serving communities in the old Latin rite, parents and catechists in this movement, educators in their schools, and parish group leaders are in fact following all the

---

35   John Pepino, "*Ex Oriente lux,*" 92–93.
36   John Paul II, "Address to the plenary assembly of the Congregation for Divine Worship and the Discipline of the Sacraments on September 21, 2001," *Adoremus Bulletin* 7.9 (December 2001–January 2002), available at https://adoremus.org/2001/12/pope-john-paul-ii-addresses-liturgical-assembly/ [accessed 2/11/2024].

"traditional pedagogies of the faith." One may well say that they live the relationship between doctrine, spirituality, apostolate, and discipline within the framework of the Latin tradition prior to the changes of the sixties and seventies. But they do so—this is worth stressing—in a wide *diversity*, and—as we have already mentioned—with a great deal of *inventiveness* to match the demands of the present-day context.

This translates into attention paid to the doctrinal content of the faith, with a concern *for catechetical transmission* in which learning has its rightful place; into a *spirituality* that emphasizes the importance of the state of grace, of the primacy of contemplation, and of the last things; into an effort to understand and appreciate the cultural and faith legacy of previous centuries, a *"filial piety towards the historical being of the Church."*[37] Through an *apostolate* that does not shy away from the explicit proclamation of Jesus Christ, the only Savior. The motto of the Chartres pilgrimage organized each year since 1983 by the Notre-Dame de Chrétienté association sums it up as follows: "Tradition, Christendom, Mission."

Cardinal Castillon Hoyos, President of the Pontifical Commission *Ecclesia Dei* from 2000 to 2009, described this world from the point of view of a prelate who was not a traditionalist, but who had come to know this group of faithful:

> I don't like, indeed, those views that would like to reduce the traditionalist "phenomenon" to only the celebration of the old rite, as if it were a stubborn and nostalgic attachment to the past. That does not correspond to the reality that it is lived within this vast group of faithful. In reality, what we frequently find is *a Christian view of the life of faith and of devotion*—shared by so many Catholic families that frequently are enriched by many

---

3 7   To use a favorite expression of Jean Madiran's. He directed the review *Itinéraires* 1956–2008 and deeply influenced "traditionalist" circles.

children—*that has special characteristics*, and we can
mention as examples: a strong sense of belonging
to the Mystical Body of Christ, a desire to maintain strong links with the past—that wishes to
be seen, not in contrast with the present but in a
line of continuity with the Church—to preserve
the principal teachings of the Faith, a profound
desire for spirituality and the sacred, etc. The love
for the Lord and for the Church, finds within
the particular Christian views of these faithful
its highest expression through their attachment
to the ancient liturgical and devotional forms
that have accompanied the Church through the
centuries of her history.[38]

3. It is also useful to look at how the "earlier forms of
the Latin tradition" are practiced in the institutes set up
by the Pontifical Commission *Ecclesia Dei*. Here, I should
like to emphasize the commonalities found among those
more directly dedicated to pastoral care.[39] These institutes
are very different in many respects—and one can only
rejoice in this as a mark of a healthy ecclesiality.

All three, however, share the following:

—a strong emphasis on the *sacramental sanctification* of
the faithful (centered on the Holy Sacrifice of the Mass),

—a *priestly formation* that is truly *Thomistic*,

—and a *priestly discipline* supported by the classic exercises
of piety enshrined in proper law (rosary, mental prayer)
and the visibility of the habitually-worn cassock.

Thanks be to God, these elements are not found only
among traditionalists. But the *conjunction* of these three
salient points, together with the liturgical specificity of
these institutes, forms a specific synthesis and marks a
singular *ethos* of the members of these institutes. This
gives them a precise character and distinguishes them

---

38 Interview with Cardinal Castrillón Hoyos granted on May 5,
2004, *The Latin Mass* 13.2 (Spring 2004): 5-6.
39 The Priestly Fraternity of St. Peter, the Institute of Christ
the King Sovereign Priest, and the Institute of the Good Shepherd.

enough for it to be recognized and protected as one of the Church's riches.

B. ECCLESIAL FITTINGNESS OF A DEDICATED ECCLESIASTICAL CIRCUMSCRIPTION

Throughout her long history, the Church has always demonstrated a surprising combination of firmness and healthy pragmatism. While leaving the fundamental elements of ecclesial communion untouched,[40] she has shown herself to be extremely inventive in resolving all kinds of specific cases.

The Church may take her time, but she always overcomes difficulties. The insertion of the Mendicant Orders into the ecclesial fabric of the Middle Ages in the thirteenth century is a case in point. There were (sometimes violent) controversies, attacks and counterattacks by interested parties, favorable measures from the Holy See followed by highly restrictive ones: the issue was hotly debated for seventy years until it was settled in a stable solution which has substantially given satisfaction for seven centuries. The comparison with our case relates, of course, to the duration and difficulty of the resolution, not to its nature.

The case of Catholic faithful legitimately attached to the "earlier forms of the Latin tradition" has yet to find a stable settlement. This group has existed for over half a century. Those who thought that it would die out as its old "nostalgic" members aged out, or through prohibition, or through attrition caused by lengthy and petty restrictions, must have noticed that such is not the case. On the contrary, the "traditionalist network" is attracting many young people[41] and has grown significantly since

---

40   See Vatican II, Decree *Unitatis redintregratio* 4, quoted in epitaph above.

41   As shown by the growing success of the Notre-Dame de Chrétienté pilgrimage each year to Chartres, where the average age is 20 or 21.

the restrictions of the last two years. It persists in its dual attachment: both to the Holy See and to "earlier forms of Latin tradition." At the same time, these faithful and these institutes are often not welcomed in diocesan pastoral ministry for who they are.

The creation of dedicated ecclesiastical circumscriptions could move things forward in the direction of stability, peace, and unity. The ambition expressed by Benedict XVI in *Summorum pontificum* was to give the "extraordinary form" its rightful place *within the very structures of the dioceses*. Some felt that the distinction of the Latin rite into two *forms* was doctrinally questionable. But pragmatically, *Summorum pontificum* was an appropriate and a decisive step forward. It has borne considerable fruit, enabling a notable expansion in the number of places where this form is celebrated, influencing the faithful in the way they participate in the Mass (e.g., by kneeling), and giving many priests of the rite of Paul VI the opportunity to discover and appreciate it.

Pope Francis has put an end to this step forward; while one may deplore this, it remains a fact. But, rather than mourning what might have been, it is more constructive now to propose something stable to the Catholic faithful legitimately attached to the "earlier forms of the Latin tradition." It seems to me that this group should be represented *in the hierarchy itself*, rather than spending its time negotiating its status with prelates, bishops, or parish priests who either have trouble understanding it or fear for the peace of their dioceses if they show favor towards it.

Given the specific nature of this group and the experience of its history over several decades, it would be natural for it to be under the authority of pastors endowed with the episcopal character. It would also be appropriate, from the point of view of well-understood pastoral practice, for these bishops to be drawn from the groups they would be called to lead. These bishops would be responsible for relations with the Holy See and other ordinaries. This would make it easier to use the pontifical and rituals in force in 1962 (ordinations, confirmations, consecration of virgins, altars and churches, etc.), while at the same time lightening the burden for bishops unaccustomed to these books and anxious not to alienate a sometimes reluctant presbyterate. Because of the episcopal charism and the sense of communion of the college of bishops, this would be a guarantee of doctrinal accuracy and pastoral prudence.[42] When it comes to establishing places of worship, these bishops dedicated to the old Latin rite could discuss conditions with other Ordinaries on equal footing. They would relieve them of the sometimes onerous task of managing these places.

The feeling that their legitimate aspirations are being recognized on a permanent basis would be beneficial to the priests and faithful of such circumscriptions. It would ease the tension. It would also, in my opinion, encourage genuine reflection on the recent magisterium, leaving aside any pragmatic aim to justify contentious dealings with a recalcitrant hierarchy. How can one calmly address the question of the status and authority of the Second Vatican Council, when it is too often invoked—counterintuitively—to justify the obligatory abolition of earlier forms?

Since these circumscriptions would have cumulative jurisdiction, the faithful would not be cut off from their dioceses of residence, and would maintain contact with the local Ordinaries. The latter would no longer be preoccupied with avoiding criticism (notably from the progressive media and part of their presbyterate) about the place they do or do not give to the old Latin rite *in their dioceses*.

For the universal Church, the existence of these circumscriptions would be indisputable proof that it does

---

42   See St. Irenaeus, *Against Heresies* 4.26.2, which speaks of "the certain charism of truth" received by the bishops through apostolic succession; see also Vatican II, *Lumen gentium*, 20.

not intend to renounce an important part of its past. The post-conciliar reforms (which have been more or less successful in and of themselves and in their application) would no longer be seen as taking precedence over union in faith and over hierarchical communion. It would also demonstrate that the magisterial texts on which the reforms claim to be based were not, *in substance*, intended to create a rupture. This is the case even though several of these texts, because of their lack of precision or the aims of some of those who conceived and applied them, have provided a basis for setting aside traditional forms.

In this respect, I think that the existence of traditional ecclesiastical circumscriptions would make it easier to draw the necessary *distinctions* between, on the one hand, the *Acts promulgated* by the Council and, on the other, certain doctrines or trends that followed them; as well as between the reforms themselves and the application of these reforms. These distinctions are often sorely lacking, both on the part of traditionalist critics and on the part of the authorities.

Cardinal Daniélou, S. J., a reformist before and during the Council, pointed this out in 1971, in his preface to the French version of a famous book by Dietrich von Hildebrand, a German philosopher much esteemed by Pius XII, St. John Paul II, and Benedict XVI:

> The particular interest of Hildebrand's book is that it doesn't just express a general attitude. It constitutes a veritable repertoire. First of all, following in the footsteps of Fr. de Lubac, he underlines the extent to which certain slogans have little basis in the Vatican II Council. The trick is to present them as the thinking of the conciliar Church, even if it means saying that out of necessity, the Council remained content with half-measures, and to accuse those who

do not follow them of not being faithful to the
Council.[43]

Moreover, the creation of such circumscriptions and
the ensuing relaxation of tensions would facilitate the
serene consideration of the different degrees of authority
of the various texts of the Council itself, and the margin
for legitimate criticism some of them allow for. It is
noteworthy that Father Bernard Lucien's work on this
point[44] received a very favorable reception in the spring
of 2012, not only in the Holy See at the Congregation for
the Doctrine of the Faith, but also from several French
cardinals and bishops. Most significant was the reaction of
the then Superior General of the SSPX, Bishop Bernard
Fellay: "This study will certainly contribute to advancing
the debate on the Second Vatican Council, I am delighted
about it and I thank you for bringing it to my attention."[45]

The Ordinaries of such ecclesiastical circumscriptions
would be in a position to discuss these issues with other
bishops and the Holy See, and they would be listened to
more effectively than ordinary priests and lay faithful. This
would be a win-win situation. Pastors would realize that
one cannot focus solely on one council without taking into
account its predecessors, without considering continuity
with the previous magisterium, and without taking into
account the authentic documents that interpret it.

---

43   Dietrich von Hildebrand, *Le cheval de Troie dans la cité de Dieu*, N.
Boyer trans. (Paris: Beauchesne, 1971), 7. [Cardinal John O'Connor
said much the same in his preface to the English edition: "It is not
unfair to say that such efforts (to establish a 'new Church') have
exploited the Council and have disguised themselves as authentic
interpretations of the Council...." *The Trojan Horse in the City of
God* (Manchester, NH: Sophia Press, 1993), x—*trans.*] See also Louis
Salleron, "Reparlons du concile," *La Pensée catholique* (Septembre-Octo-
bre 1977).

44   Bernard Lucien, "The Magisterial Authority of Vatican II: A
Contribution to an Ongoing Debate," David M. Foley trans., *Sedes
Sapientiæ* Special English-Language Issue (2022): 21–90, originally
published as "L'autorité magistérielle de Vatican II. Contribution à
un débat actuel," *Sedes Sapientiæ* 119 (March 2012): 9–80.

45   Letter dated April 16, 2012.

An alternative solution

Since the publication of *Traditionis custodes*, the situation has been stuck in a painful deadlock. For the bishops, some of the measures of this motu proprio are virtually impossible to apply, such as the prohibition, as specified by the *Dubia* of December 2021, of authorizing the habitual celebration of the traditional rite in parishes. A dispassionate analysis must also take into account the fact that the results of the April 2020 survey of bishops worldwide on the application of *Summorum pontificum* have not been made public, and that what was presented to the Holy Father, according to senior prelates, did not reflect the reality of the situation. In any case, the considerations set out in the accompanying letter apply only to a very narrow margin of the faithful.

It would therefore be natural for the hierarchy and these faithful to ask the Holy Father to repeal or substantially modify this text, and above all to make the sacraments in the old rite available to the faithful once again, with the erection of *personal parishes*.

As early as 1997, the superiors of the *Ecclesia Dei* communities stressed the importance of this personal parish structure, suggesting that "the Holy See invites Ordinaries to respond favorably to the requests of the faithful, by erecting personal parishes for these same rites (cf. can. 518). In these parishes, the sensibility, not only liturgical, but also spiritual and disciplinary, of the faithful will be respected (see motu proprio *Ecclesia Dei*, 5c and 6a)."[46]

Absent the creation of an ecclesiastical circumscription, one could also take up an idea already considered in discussions with the *Ecclesia Dei* Commission, namely the appointment of a pontifical delegate to deal with the application of the Holy See's measures by the bishops. It would, moreover, be highly desirable for this delegate to

---

46   Memorandum dated May 30, 1997 signed by the superiors of the FSSP, the ICKSP, the FSVF, and by the abbots of Le Barroux and the Canons Regular of the Mother of God (Lagrasse), 5.

have episcopal status, as this would enable him speak with the Ordinaries on an equal footing.

The solution proposed in this article, an ecclesiastical circumscription dedicated to the old Latin rite, is simply a possible alternative to get out of a seemingly hopeless situation. It is also in line with the Decree of February 11, 2022 granted to the Priestly Fraternity of St. Peter, which more systematically makes room for proper law within general law.

This would not be the first time in the history of the Church that the law has evolved along with the experience and legitimate wishes of the faithful. All the more so since the current emphasis on synodality invites us to take greater account of their aspirations.

Thoughts on a Possible Traditional Ordinariate

JOSEPH SHAW

F R. LOUIS-MARIE DE BLIGNIÈRES HAS done us a service by raising once again the question of an "ordinariate" or other kind of *circumscriptio* or circumscription as a way forward for the traditional movement and the Traditional Latin Mass (TLM).[1]

A "circumscription" in ordinary English usage is simply a defined area, but in canon law it is a community of faithful governed by an "ordinary," which is circumscribed in terms of a group of people and/or geography, like a chaplaincy but on a larger scale. Examples are military ordinariates, the Ordinariates used by the former Anglicans, the Prelature formerly enjoyed by Opus Dei, the Exarchates for members of Eastern Churches living in the West, and the Apostolic Administration of St. John Vianney in Campos, Brazil, under Bishop Rifan. Exactly how it relates to geographical dioceses would depend upon the small print of its founding statutes, but this legal structure implies a few things.

Lay members of a Traditionalist Ordinariate (as I shall call it) could also be members of a geographical diocese.

It would have dedicated priestly members, who would answer to the head of the Ordinariate, the Ordinary. It could borrow priests from dioceses (like military ordinariates), and/or it could have its own seminary; it could also be home to religious communities and priestly Institutes.

---

1   See Fr. de Blignières' preceding article.

Fr. de Blignières assumes the Ordinary would be a bishop, but the Anglican Ordinariates generally have a priest, who is nevertheless entitled to some of the privileges of a bishop (ring, pectoral cross, etc., as well as membership of the Bishops' Conference).

Such an ordinariate could have a distinct liturgical expression and a particular law.

There could either be one world-wide (like the Opus Dei Prelature), or a number of ordinariates serving the same group of people in different regions (like the former Anglicans), or one for each Bishops' Conference (like military ordinariates), or one in each of those conferences that needed one (like the Exarchates for Greek Catholics). Fr. de Blignières has in mind not a world-wide Ordinariate, but one covering, for example, France.

Clearly this legal structure has its usefulness, since there are a good number of them and they seem to work as intended. Leaving Opus Dei's former Prelature aside, since it has been abolished, why do some laity and priests need a structure like this?

Military ordinariates are necessary because Catholics in the armed services need priests who can be deployed when they are deployed: a dedicated team. Exarchates for the Eastern Rites need a specialist clergy for a quite different reason: to serve a community with a distinct liturgical heritage who are governed by a distinct discipline (on fasting, for example). Less obvious is the case of the Anglican converts, but the hope of them maintaining an 'Anglican patrimony' depends on their maintaining a distinct identity.

The Apostolic Administration of Campos is not difficult to fit into this pattern, and it is clear that a case could be made for a traditionalist ordinariate serving other countries: a distinct liturgy can be served by a distinct group of priests answerable to a special Ordinary.

A "Traditional Ordinariate" or "Apostolic Prelature" was formally proposed to the then Cardinal Joseph Ratzinger by Una Voce International (FIUV) in 1990, and it was raised again in the same year by Dom Gérard Calvet of Le Barroux in a meeting with Pope John Paul II.

It was not taken up in Pope Benedict's Apostolic Letter *Summorum pontificum* (SP) in 2007, but arose once more in the context of the project to reconcile the Society of St. Pius X. The practical plan for the reconciliation, which seems to have been accepted by both sides in around 2012, apparently involved an Ordinariate structure. It is perhaps no coincidence that Ordinariates for former Anglicans had been set up in 2010. However, this attempt at reconciliation failed for other reasons and the details were never confirmed.

The prospect of an Ordinariate created for the SSPX raised the question of how the "Ecclesia Dei groups," the other traditional priestly institutes and communities, would relate to it. It might appeal to the tidy-minded to have them all in the same structure, but if the Ordinariate were dominated by, or even run by, the SSPX, it would not be surprising if other institutes and communities would be less enthusiastic about being subject to it. I will consider below the case of priests and communities who use both Missals.

We are now in different circumstances, but if the Holy See took a more positive view of the TLM, making an Ordinariate a real possibility, the question becomes one of whether we should be asking for an Ordinariate or a return to something along the likes of SP, or if that is too ambitious, then the situation created by Pope John Paul II's Apostolic Letter *Ecclesia Dei* (ED) in 1988.

The advantages and disadvantages of an Ordinariate seem to me as follows.

PLACES OF WORSHIP

A new Ordinariate, or one establishing itself in a new region, would not start off with its own places of worship, though assuming the Priestly Institutes and communities were part of it they might bring some with them. The

Traditionalist Ordinariate, like the Anglican Ordinariates, would have to ask for some suitable places of worship from geographical sees.

Fr. de Blignières notes that the Ordinary would be able to negotiate with bishops over churches from a position of "equality," but it is difficult to know what difference this would make. Currently, some bishops willingly make churches available for the celebration of the Traditional Mass, and others do not. Giving a church to an Ordinariate would be more like giving it (outright, or on a long lease) to one of the Institutes, than allowing a diocesan priest to use it for the TLM while he is posted there: that is, it would be harder to get it back again. However, this might make some bishops more reluctant to give them, and as we see with the former-Anglican Ordinariates, it is possible for bishops to offer church-sharing arrangements with an Ordinariate, just as they might to make provision for the TLM under ED or SP.

LAITY

Presumably, any member of the Faithful could attend services offered by the Ordinariate, and having weddings and baptisms and so on would require no more than some kind of formal registration. The Ordinariate would, again presumably, offer a full set of sacraments, blessings, catechism and so on, as the Institutes do today, but this does not mean that these things would be any easier to find, because the existence of the legal structure does not necessarily mean that there would be more priests to offer these things or churches in which they could be offered.

One clear advantage of the structure *could*, however, be a distinct liturgical discipline—on holy days of obligation, fasting, and so on—as is the case with the Eastern Churches. A more demanding compulsory discipline of fasting and more numerous holy days will be more widely and consistently observed in the traditional community; they will therefore influence its inner life and form part of how it appears to outsiders. For these reasons, Una Voce International has argued for more rigorous obligations both for Holy Days of Obligation[2] and the Eucharistic Fast.[3]

The Ordinariate's Particular Law might or might not make a distinct discipline possible. I would guess that it probably would not, since it would be a potential source of confusion, if the laity were able to move freely between the Ordinariate and their geographical diocese, although Eastern Catholics are supposed to maintain their fasting regime even if they cannot regularly attend their own liturgy.

CLERGY

Under SP and ED, clergy of dioceses and also or communities and religious orders were able to celebrate the TLM; in the case of ED, public celebrations needed the permission of their superior or bishop. The big question for the Ordinariate proposal is whether priests who are not members would still be able to take up the TLM without joining the Ordinariate, and whether bi-ritualism would be possible, i.e., a priest habitually saying both the TLM and the Novus Ordo.

Bi-ritualism between the Use of the former-Anglican Ordinariate and the *Novus Ordo* is universal among the clergy of those Ordinariates; bi-ritualism between the Latin and Eastern Rites is less common but is certainly possible. If the object of the exercise is to remove from the shoulders of bishops the burden imposed by both ED and SP, of finding ways to accommodate, or to refuse to accommodate, priests and people who desire to celebrate or assist at the TLM, this suggests that the TLM would

---

2　See Fœderatio Internationalis Una Voce, *Positio* No. 13: Holy Days of Obligation (November 2012): https://unavoce.ru/pdf/FIUV_PP/FIUV_PP13_HolyDaysFinal3.pdf

3　See Fœderatio Internationalis Una Voce, *Positio* No. 10: The Eucharistic Fast (August 2012): https://unavoce.ru/pdf/FIUV_PP/FIUV_PP10_EucharisticFastFinal.pdf

disappear from diocesan churches and religious orders outside the Ordinariate.

There are different ways in which this last issue could be handled in the legal establishment, but if this is what happens, it would be a major disadvantage.

THE LAW OF GRADUALISM

The restriction of the TLM to the confines of a Traditionalist Ordinariate would be unfortunate for several reasons.

Members of the laity are less likely to discover the TLM if it were not found in parish churches being celebrated by priests they know. In my experience, if a diocesan priest starts a TLM in a parish, a proportion of the regular parishioners, as well newcomers, start attending it, and this proportion increases with the passage of time. These are people who would never have sought the TLM out in a special location.

Priests are less likely to try out celebrating the TLM if they cannot start by doing it occasionally as part of their parish ministry. The pattern is often that a priest starts celebrating it on a day off, then on a weekday, then on a Saturday, and then on a Sunday. If this journey of a gradually increasing attachment to the TLM is not possible, many priests will never take the plunge.

Communities and religious orders also, under ED and SP, in many cases experienced a similar gradual opening up to the TLM, with first one priest celebrating it quietly, and then another, until finally it becomes an important part of their ministry, with a major Sunday Mass. This has happened with various Oratories of St. Philip Neri, and various houses of the Dominicans. If gradualism is impossible, this process would not occur.

Bishops, too, get drawn in to the TLM, first tolerating it, then attending it in parishes or apostolates of the Traditional Institutes, and then sometimes celebrating Confirmations, Ordinations, and Masses on special occasions.

It is true that these processes were in some cases associated with conflict, and this conflict is certainly part of the reason why *Traditionis custodes* was promulgated. This is very regrettable, but the conflict is not reducible to a lack of tact by some of those drawn to the Traditional Mass. The appearance of the TLM in a parish, diocese or religious community sometimes brought to the surface a deep unwillingness on the part of some laity, priests, and bishops, to accept that the TLM is genuinely legitimate and of real value. If this kind of quiet hatred of the TLM is simply allowed to persist, then it will continue to poison the life of the Church, for the reason given by Pope Benedict XVI: it is a disavowal of the past that imperils the Church's very existence as a community. On the other hand, as we know from experience, many bishops, priests, and lay Catholics have lost their initial hostility to the TLM and its adherents simply by getting to know it and them.

I do not know how familiar Fr. de Blignières may be with the gradual processes and half-way houses that I have just described. Certainly, the distinction between the faithful in the Church attached to the TLM and those committed solely to the *Novus Ordo* must seem much more clear-cut from the perspective of the Traditional Institutes and communities than it does for those who attend the ancient Mass in a parish setting. We can argue about how satisfactory it is for a priest to celebrate both liturgical forms, or for the faithful to go from one to the other—some people think this is wonderful and enriching; others feel that there is a painful tension in this situation. But we should not see it solely as a *state of affairs:* it is also a *pipeline,* one that a great many people have passed through on the way to a deeper and richer engagement with their Catholic heritage and spirituality.

Traditionis custodes can be read as intended precisely to put a stop to these processes: we are not supposed to "promote" the TLM to members of the laity not already

in a "group" attending it; priests are restricted in start-
ing to say it; bishops are prohibited in most cases from
celebrating confirmations; and so on. At the same time,
the Traditional Institutes and communities seem to be
largely (though not entirely) immune to its effects.

If this is indeed the aim of *Traditionis custodes*—to keep
the traditionalists quarantined away from the rest of the
Church—it would not seem sensible for supporters of the
Traditional Mass to lend their support to it, by advocating
a Traditional Ordinariate.

Interview with Father de Blignières

ON AN "ECCLESIASTICAL CIRCUMSCRIPTION" FOR THE OLD LATIN RITE*

BY ELIZABETH CAILLEMER

1. Why are you proposing the creation of an "ecclesiastical circumscription" for the old Latin Rite?

Because a completely new situation has been created by the motu proprio *Traditionis custodes* of July 16, 2021, and by the documents issued by the Dicastery for Divine Worship in December 2021. These texts created a deadlock for Catholics attached to the "earlier forms of the Latin tradition"[1] and wishing to maintain hierarchical communion. Pope Francis has ended the period of relative calm that followed the motu proprio *Summorum pontificum* (2007–2021)....

Instead of mourning what might have been, we must now offer something stable to those Catholics who are loyal to the Holy See and to the traditional pedagogy of the faith. This group must constantly negotiate its status with prelates, bishops, or parish priests who often find it difficult to understand them (or fear for the peace of their dioceses if they show favouritism toward them). This situation is unsustainable in the long run: we believe that this group should be represented *in the Church hierarchy*.

* This interview was first published in French in the journal *Tu es Petrus*, n. 41 (January–February 2024), in reference to a previous article by Fr. Louis-Marie de Blignières, "Une 'circonscription ecclésiastique' pour l'ancien rite latin," in *Sedes Sapientiæ*, n. 165 (September 2023): 17–44.
1 Pope John Paul II, motu proprio *Ecclesia Dei*, July 2 1988, n. 5.

2. What does an ecclesiastical circumscription consist of?

"Ecclesiastical circumscription" is a generic term used by canonists, which encompasses a number of very different realities. Ecclesiastical circumscriptions, broadly speaking, are communities of the faithful with a clergy under the authority of a Bishop.[2] They are either dioceses (or particular churches), or entities created for special reasons, and legally assimilated to dioceses: for example, military ordinariates and personal apostolic administrations. These could serve as models for the proposal we are discussing. Vatican II encouraged the development of such structures. According to a well-known canonist, "The adaptability of ecclesiastical organization to the pastoral realities of the faithful is one of the essential aspects of the last ecumenical assembly [i.e., the Second Vatican Council]."[3]

3. Who can decide to erect such an entity? And who can request one?

The Code of Canon Law makes this clear: "It is only for the supreme authority to erect particular churches; those legitimately erected possess juridic personality by the law itself" (can. 373 § 1). This erection is therefore the responsibility of the Holy See, through the Dicastery for Bishops or, in missionary territories, the Dicastery for Evangelization. Thus, in the Decree of 18 January 2002, the Congregation for Bishops erected the Personal Apostolic Administration of *St. John Mary Vianney* in the Diocese of Campos, Brazil. Paragraph II of the Decree reads:

> To the Apostolic Administration is assigned the faculty of celebrating the Holy Eucharist, the other sacraments, the Liturgy of the Hours and other liturgical actions according to the Roman Rite and liturgical discipline prescribed

---

2   See The Catholic Church in Canada, "Ecclesiastical Circumscriptions," https://www.cccb.ca/the-catholic-church-in-canada/ecclesiastical-circumscriptions/

3   Dominique Le Tourneau, *Manuel de droit canonique* (Wilson et Lafleur: Montréal, 2012), 193.

by St. Pius V, with the modifications introduced
by his successors up to Blessed John XXIII.

4. Who can apply?

As I explain in my article, over the past thirty-five years,
requests to this effect have been made by community
superiors, individually or in groups, and by lay presidents
of associations such as *Una Voce*; the Pontifical Commission *Ecclesia Dei* has also made some similar suggestions.
The Church is not a free-for-all where anyone can claim
what he wants. From time immemorial, however, the
lay faithful and priests have presented to the hierarchy
their just intuitions, according to their own charism, for
the common good of the Church ... and the Church has
often taken them into account. In this case, it would be
a proposal to resolve a serious problem that has been
pending since the end of the Council and to contribute
to a genuine renewal in a crisis that is increasingly recognized. It would be desirable, of course, that this new
proposal should be supported by the bishops.

The Church's traditional practice is clearly set out in
the current Code:

> According to the knowledge, competence, and
> prestige which they possess, they *[i.e., the faith-
> ful]* have the right and even at times the duty
> to manifest to the sacred pastors their opinion
> on matters which pertain to the good of the
> Church and to make their opinion known to
> the rest of the Christian faithful, without prej-
> udice to the integrity of faith and morals, with
> reverence toward their pastors, and attentive to
> common advantage and the dignity of persons
> (can. 212 § 3).

5. Who would be in charge and who would appoint him? If it were a bishop chosen from among the priests of the former Ecclesia Dei communities, wouldn't the choice of one rather than another cause problems?

The Holy See also appoints the Prelate of ecclesiastical circumscriptions. Thus, for the military ordinariates:

> §1 In charge of a Military Ordinariate is placed an Ordinary as its proper authority: he will normally be a bishop, enjoying all the rights and being bound by the obligations of diocesan bishops, unless the nature of things or particular statutes require otherwise.

> §2 The Supreme Pontiff freely nominates the Military Ordinary, or institutes or confirms the candidate legitimately designated.[4]

The Ordinary of this structure could be a religious or a diocesan priest, or even an available bishop, who would have all the qualities necessary for the task, including a love of doctrine, a good knowledge of traditional rites and the confidence of his flock. In our view there is no shortage of such men. If the Ordinary is a priest from a former *Ecclesia Dei* institute, his appointment will benefit everyone. It will be appropriate to set aside personal preferences, however legitimate, and look to the common good of the Church. As we saw in February 2022, the decree obtained in favour of the Priestly Fraternity of St. Peter changed the atmosphere and, by applying the principle of canonical analogy, benefited all the Institutes.

6. How would its prerogatives relate to those of the diocesan bishops?

In military ordinariates and personal apostolic administrations, the faithful do not cease to belong to their diocese of origin, according to their place of residence. There is a so-called "cumulative jurisdiction" of the local Bishop and the Prelate of the Ordinariate, the conditions of which are specified in the Statutes of the Ordinariate.

---

4   Pope John Paul II, Apostolic Constitution *Spirituali Militum Curæ*, April 21, 1986, II, §§ 1 and 2.

7. How do I become a member? Can I belong to both an ecclesiastical circumscription and my diocese?

Yes, because of cumulative jurisdiction, the faithful belong to both structures. In the case of the personal apostolic administration, "membership is by inscription in an *ad hoc* register of the faithful who wish to be included."[5]

8. How would the faithful of the Old Rite obtain places of worship?

Existing places of worship would have no reason to disappear. They would continue to function as they do now, if the local Ordinary prefers this solution. They would be taken over by the circumscription if the Ordinary so wished. In this case the priests who serve them, if they are diocesan, could be attached to the circumscription by being incardinated into it. If they are members of an institute, agreements would be signed between the circumscription and the institute, as is currently the case with local Ordinaries.

For the opening of new places of worship, the Prelate of the Circumscription, who is a Bishop, will have more leverage to negotiate with the local Ordinaries. And the latter will be all the more inclined to give the green light, since they will not have the heavy burden of serving and administering these places.

9. Would this structure allow priests to celebrate all the sacraments according to the Vetus Ordo *without conditions?*

Yes, of course, that is precisely its purpose. See the decree for Campos quoted above.

10. Where would the clergy of this ecclesiastical district come from?

The recommended district would be able to accommodate diocesan priests who wish to devote themselves to an apostolate based on traditional pedagogy. There are undoubtedly more of them than one might imagine.

5　Le Tourneau, *Manuel de droit canonique*, 200.

It could also set up its own seminary to train incardinated clergy.

> These [personal ecclesiastical] circumscriptions belong to the hierarchical organization of the Church: they therefore have a church which is the see of the ordinary or prelate, a curia, possibly a seminary of their own and a tribunal of their own, etc.[6]

The former *Ecclesia Dei* institutes will certainly be eager to help the ecclesiastical circumscription by offering teachers to train seminarians. Some young men may have a genuine clerical vocation in the traditional rites without having one that corresponds to the particular charisms of these Societies of Apostolic Life, which are the Priestly Fraternity of St. Peter, the Institute of Christ the King Sovereign Priest and the Institute of the Good Shepherd. Since the harvest is abundant, let us rejoice that these young people can find a suitable setting for the greater good of the faithful.

11. Why would Rome agree to set up such an entity when it is seeking to do away with the Old Rite?

The answer to your question must take into account the long history of the Church. On the one hand, despite the famous letter accompanying *Traditionis custodes*, the will of "Rome" is not very clear. The position of Archbishop Arthur Roche's Dicastery for Divine Worship is clearly in favour of the abolition of traditional rites. But he is unable to obtain a decisive text from the Holy Father, who seems less concerned about this issue since his decree in favour of the Priestly Fraternity of St. Peter. For the time being, the Dicastery for Religious is confining itself to its task of supervising the conformity of the life of the members of religious institutes with their constitutions.

On the other hand, we need to be cautious when making pessimistic prognostications about the future of

---

6   Le Tourneau, *Manuel de droit canonique*, 198.

the Church. On May 24, 1976, when Paul VI vigorously expressed the prohibition of the Traditional Roman Rite, who would have predicted that on July 7, 2007, his successor would restore this rite to its rightful place in society, stating further that "because of its venerable and ancient usage, it must enjoy the honour due to it and ... that it has never been abrogated"?[7]

In the Church there are never good reasons to give in to definitive despair. Will the solution we propose be implemented during the pontificate of Pope Francis? Perhaps not, but how can we present this as a certainty? If it were, it would not be the first surprise the Holy Father has in store for us, after the facilities granted in 2016 and 2017 to the Priestly Society of St. Pius X and the decree of 2022 for the Priestly Society of St. Peter. It is significant that Father Henri Donneaud, O. P., who wrote an article against the maintenance of the old Roman rite in dioceses, considers at the same time that a dedicated ecclesiastical circumscription would be a possible solution to the crisis.[8] "There is a legitimate place for a plurality of rites in the Latin Church, insofar as each of them expresses in the liturgy the specific cultural and spiritual traits of a particular Church or religious family."[9]

12. Which members of the faithful already benefit from such an organization within the Church?

The *Annuario Pontificio* 2023 includes just one Personal Apostolic Administration, that of Campos, which we have already mentioned, and the three Personal Ordinariates for former Anglicans erected by Benedict XVI in 2011 and 2012.

---

7   Pope Benedict XVI, motu proprio *Summorum pontificum*, art. 1.
8   "In a spirit of pacification, you propose a profound solution, from the heart of the Gospel, I would say" (Letter to the author from Father Donneaud, December 21, 2021).
9   Henri Donneaud, O. P., "Le pape François, garant de la doctrine liturgique de Saint Pie V," *Nouvelle revue théologique*, n. 144 (January-March 2022), 48.

13. Would such an organization be more permanent than a motu proprio? Is it more permanent than a personal prelature, which has recently been eviscerated by Rome?

Your question reflects the mistrust that has built up in traditional circles since the beginning of the Church's long crisis. In 1988, the Priestly Society of St. Pius X reiterated that our *Ecclesia Dei* institutes would be suppressed very quickly, but they have continued to exist and grow for thirty-five years... Apart from the divine hierarchical structure formed by the bishops as successors of the apostles and by the primacy of Peter and his successors, no canonical entity in the Catholic Church (not even the concrete boundaries of dioceses) has the promise of eternity. Nor, of course, does the stable structure we advocate! But it is a well-recognized canonical configuration that must and can endure as long as the causes that led to its establishment and the good it does the Church remain.

> Canon 368. Particular churches, in which and from which the one and only Catholic Church exists, are first of all dioceses, to which, unless it is otherwise evident, are likened a territorial prelature and territorial abbacy, an apostolic vicariate and an apostolic prefecture, and an apostolic administration erected in a stable manner.
>
> Canon 371 § 2. An apostolic administration is a certain portion of the people of God which is not erected as a diocese by the Supreme Pontiff due to special and particularly grave reasons and whose pastoral care is entrusted to an apostolic administrator who governs it in the name of the Supreme Pontiff.

The "particularly grave reasons" for erecting the recommended circumscription are not only to put an end to the sidelining of traditional pedagogies, but to give them a stable, peaceful framework in which to practice, relieving the diocesan bishops and ensuring the peace of the Church. This can extend over a very long period of time.

14. Would belonging to this entity harm the unity of the Church? Can you remind us of the criteria for ecclesial communion?

Faced with the abuse of this notion, I have been led in several contributions to recall the true criteria of communion.[10]

> The notion of *communion*, as it is widely lived in the Church today, seems marked by a shift from *intelligible content* (received through faith, informed by sacramental charity, structured by law) to the *existential experience* of the group: in essence, by a shift from the primacy of truth to that of unity. This kind of communion is certainly linked to certain aspects of modernity, which dislikes the intelligible, and favors the group, the instantaneous and the emotional. But it is also one of the expressions of the crisis in the Church.[11]

The criteria for Catholic communion are the profession of faith, recognition of the seven sacraments in their various rites, and hierarchical communion with the bishops as successors of the Apostles and with the Pope.

15. If Rome were to agree to set up such a structure for the old Latin rite, would this not be a kind of disavowal of the 1969 liturgical reform?

Not necessarily. The argument of disavowal is that of the unconditional supporters of the reform, who see in the Old Rite inadmissible competition for the reformed rite. But some bishops and priests (in growing numbers) are aware that the reform promulgated by Paul VI is not "the mass of Vatican II," contrary to what some (progressive or traditionalist) repeat. They will be delighted that the Latin Church has a liturgical point of reference that enables them to celebrate Masses according to the

---

10   For example: "De la 'communion' et de la crise dans l'Église," *Sedes Sapientiæ*, n. 113 (September 2010); "La communion dans tous ses états," *Sedes Sapientiæ*, n. 130 (December 2014); "Le pape et le droit propre des religieux," *Sedes Sapientiæ*, n. 159 (March 2022).
11   "De la 'communion' et de la crise dans l'Église," 10.

reformed rite in line with the Council's indications in *Sacrosanctum concilium.*

16. Do you think that the creation of this ecclesiastical circum-scription would relieve the diocesan bishops, who are sometimes forced by their collaborators to be harsh with traditionalists?

Yes, undeniably. And by contrast, some bishops, con-cerned that these faithful should not leave their juris-diction, will be more willing to welcome them as they are within the diocesan framework, and this will also be positive.

17. What other solutions do you propose to overcome this crisis?

The repealing of *Traditionis custodes* and a return to *Summorum pontificum,* but with the systematic creation of the personal parishes recommended by this latter motu proprio (art. 10).

18. How can this be achieved?

Through the normal channels: bishops, theologians, and "healthy Catholic public opinion," in the words of Pius XII. We should ask help from those bishops who realize the great scandal that *Traditionis custodes* has caused for many of their faithful, and not just for traditionalists. Exasperated by the petty control measures imposed by the Dicastery for Divine Worship, they yearn for a return to the relative peace of pre-2021. One way of facilitating this would be the full publication of the preliminary investigation, which we know was largely in favour of maintaining *Summorum pontificum.* We also need to encourage theological studies that are increasingly undermining the progressive ideology in liturgical matters, and that demonstrate the doctrinal and pastoral importance of traditional pedagogies of faith in a disintegrating Western world.

19. To justify a legal evolution in the situation of traditionalists, you say that it would not be the first time in the history of the Church

that the law evolved in line with the wishes of the faithful. What are some examples of this?

In my article, I take the example of the status of the Mendicant Orders.[12] [...] It is also important to note that a significant period of time was required (from Pius IX to the Second Vatican Council) to provide the Eastern Catholic rites with a juridical configuration that corresponded to their rightful place in the Catholic Church. As a final example, we may cite the development of liturgical and disciplinary rules concerning the adoration of the Blessed Sacrament and Eucharistic Communion.

20. Tailor-made structures have been granted by Rome to certain groups to encourage their integration into the Church (certain Eastern Churches, Anglicans, etc.). Isn't the case of the traditionalist faithful different, in that they are already in the Church?

Of course it is! Church law is geared to the salvation of souls, and is imaginative when necessary. It is not univocally stuck on one formula or another, and it creates structures that respond to new needs.[13] Benedict XVI has wisely encouraged the return of Anglicans to full communion through the new personal ordinariates. The grave situation created by the crisis in the Church (and especially by the decades-long prohibition and persecution of traditional rites) is new. Given its gravity, it requires an original approach. I am sure that Pope Francis, or one of his successors, will have the opportunity to be creative with traditional pedagogies of faith, certainly for reasons other than simply reintegration into communion—ultimately, this solution could be directed towards the deployment of all Catholic forces for the evangelization of a world submerged by materialistic technocracy.

---

12   See Fr. de Blignières' article in this volume.
13   Cf. can. 372 § 2: "Nevertheless, where in the judgment of the supreme authority of the Church it seems advantageous after the conferences of bishops concerned have been heard, particular churches distinguished by the rite of the faithful or some other similar reason can be erected in the same territory."

A Look Back at the Consecrations of June 30, 1988

JOSEPH BISIG, FSSP
Co-founder of the Priestly Fraternity of St. Peter

LOUIS-MARIE DE BLIGNIÈRES, FSVF
Founder of the Fraternity of St. Vincent Ferrer

SEPTEMBER 22, 2022

W E EXPRESS OUR THANKS TO FR. Jean-Michel Gleize, SSPX, who has recently restated the position of the Society of St. Pius X on the legitimacy of the consecrations conferred on June 30, 1988 without a pontifical mandate,[1] which gives us the opportunity to return to this important question. Having experienced firsthand what preceded and followed these consecrations, we decided in the summer of 1988 to live in full fidelity to the rites of the Latin tradition within the hierarchical communion. We then experienced the painful separation from Archbishop Marcel Lefebvre, who ordained us in 1977 and whose great priestly and missionary spirit always edified us.

We are both founders of Fraternities canonically erected by the Holy See in October 1988. Archbishop Lefebvre and many of the priests who followed him predicted that our

---

1   In three articles published in the *Courrier de Rome* 655 (July-August 2022): "Pie XII et l'épiscopat," 1–5; "L'Opinion commune des théologiens sur l'épiscopat," 5–9; "La Fraternité Saint Pierre et l'épiscopat," 10–12.

Fraternities would not remain faithful to their founding acts, that we would be contaminated by "modernism," and that we would eventually be suppressed within a short time. The past thirty-four years have shown the inaccuracy of these predictions. Both of our institutes, in spite of various pressures, both internal and external, have remained faithful to their original *raison d'être*. In spite of much opposition, they have undergone significant growth. This point sheds a telling light on what those who favor the consecrations call "survival operation": the 1988 consecrations were, they say, absolutely necessary for "the Tradition" to survive. Our existence proves just the opposite.

Let us return to the basic reasons for our disagreement with the 1988 consecrations and our rejection of the separation from the Catholic hierarchy that followed and has continued ever since.

Fr. Gleize affirms that our reflection is "devoid of any foundation in the data of Tradition."[2] We invite the reader who would like to verify the validity of this assertion to refer to our studies at the time, which are now available online.[3] He will see that they are abundantly and solidly founded on the doctrine of the Fathers and on the Magisterium. Here, we restrict ourselves to highlighting what is opposed to Fr. Gleize's assertions in his most recent work.

His approach may be outlined as follows.

Fr. Gleize insists on the difference in nature, in the episcopate, between the power of order (transmitted by the sacred rites of consecration) and the power of jurisdiction

---

2   *Ibid.*, 12.
3   Louis-Marie de Blignières, "Réflexions sur l'épiscopat *autonome*," *Sedes Sapientiæ*, Supplément doctrinal n. 2 (June 1987); Fr. Josef Bisig (ed.), "Du sacre épiscopal contre la volonté du pape, avec application aux sacres conférés le 30 juin par Mgr Lefebvre," a collaborative essay by FSSP members (n.d.: early 1989). The first article is available at: https://www.chemere.org/blog/2022/9/30/du-sacre-episcopal-contre-la-volonte-du-pape; and the second, at: https://www.chemere.org/blog/2022/9/30/etude-episcopat-autonome

(transmitted by the injunction of the Supreme Pontiff). He affirms a "perfect separability" of these two powers.

Schism, in this view, consists only in wanting to transmit the power of jurisdiction without the pope's consent, as the Chinese bishops did in the 1950s. The pure transmission of the power of order then constitutes at most a disobedience, and it is justified in certain cases of necessity. Archbishop Lefebvre, on June 30, 1988, denied that he was transmitting any jurisdiction whatsoever and considered that there was a case of necessity: "His goal was to give Tradition and the Church the means to perpetuate the priesthood, without compromising with the novelties of Vatican II."[4]

This reasoning is invalidated by several considerations.

1. Let us hypothetically grant the "perfect separability" of order and jurisdiction. It is worth noting that Fr. Gleize omits to mention that, in a legitimate consecration, the exercise of jurisdiction always intervenes. Indeed, the act by which the Pope designates the subject to be consecrated does not belong to the power of order, but to the government of the Church. A bishop who ordains a priest not designated by the Pope, even if he does not intend to pass on to that priest any jurisdiction, is indeed usurping the Pope's jurisdiction by choosing that priest as his bishop. This is disobedience in a grave matter and, according to the criterion put forward by Fr. Gleize (i.e., schism is only in the usurpation of jurisdiction), it is indeed a schismatic act.

2. The perfect separability of which Fr. Gleize speaks must be nuanced. It is true that there are bishops who do not have actual jurisdiction, but all of them (unlike simple priests) have, in virtue of their consecration, an aptitude of divine right for this jurisdiction. There is, in the episcopal dignity itself, a relationship to the Mystical Body, which is not reducible to the power of ordaining

---

4   Gleize, "L'Opinion," 9.

and confirming the baptized. This relationship concerns the very *regency* of the Church, including in this notion the power to teach and to govern. This power becomes jurisdiction only through the designation of subjects. However, it calls for this designation; it is intrinsically ordered to it by the very will of Christ, so much so that the ordering to jurisdiction (of the external forum) is part of the very notion of the episcopate. "It would be a contradiction in terms to conceive of a consecrated bishop who did not have, in the character itself, any relation to the government of the Church."[5] This truth is independent of the question of the sacramentality of the episcopate.

He who receives the episcopate without an apostolic mandate thus receives a spiritual power intrinsically ordered to the government of the Church, yet without any injunction from those who have authority in the Church. He receives a power essentially ordered to an act reserved, by divine right, to those in authority in the Church. This is a serious vitiation, which is, if not schismatic, at least in the very line of schism. This is why Pius XII describes the consecration received without the apostolic institution as "a serious attack on the very unity of the Church."[6]

The same Pope expresses very clearly the illegitimacy of a consecration without a pontifical mandate: "No one can legitimately confer episcopal consecration without the prior certainty of a pontifical mandate."[7] Fr. Gleize quotes this passage without clarifying its meaning, which is nevertheless obvious.[8]

---

5   Camillo Mazzella, *De Religione et Ecclesia* (Rome, 1880), 788. Fr. de Blignières, in "Réflexions sur l'épiscopat *autonome*," 26–28n33, quotes seventeen classical theologians who mention this relationship of the bishop to the government of the Church.
6   Pope Pius XII, Encyclical *Ad Apostolorum Principis*, June 29, 1958, AAS 50 (1958), 612, in *Osservatore Romano*, 8–9 September 1958; reprinted in St. Maurice Edition (1958), 337.
7   *Ibid.*
8   Gleize, "Pie XII," 4.

3. Schism occurs when consecrations are made with the intention of withdrawing from pontifical jurisdiction or from communion of the universal Church. This was the case for the constitution of the Chinese "Patriotic Church." This is what happened with the consecrations of June 30, 1988. Archbishop Lefebvre did not intend to *transmit* a jurisdiction but to *withdraw* from one. This is what emerges from the principal motive recalled by Fr. Gleize: to evade the "modernist authorities," to carry out a survival operation of "Tradition" outside of the hierarchical structures.[9]

That is why John Paul II, in the motu proprio *Ecclesia Dei*, rightly spoke of a "schismatic act." It was clear to all that it was not only a question of promoting a few priests to the episcopate, but the stated goal of this act was to take the means to dispense the sacraments and teaching *independently from the Catholic hierarchy, the Pope, and the bishops in communion with him.*

In fact, since 1988, the SSPX has *officially* behaved as if it had no subordination to the Catholic hierarchy.[10] It has intensified this attitude since 2018. No authorization (apart from what is physically indispensable, such as the use of a basilica for a pilgrimage) is requested for any pastoral, apostolic, or teaching activity. No directive from the hierarchy as such is followed.[11] No document from the Magisterium after 1962 is received. Such documents are sometimes criticized all the more for containing good elements that might be "traps" (e.g., the *Catechism of the Catholic Church, Veritatis splendor, Dominus Jesus*).

More serious yet is the fact that the SSPX grants dispensations from marriage impediments and judges the

---

9   Gleize, "La Fraternité Saint Pierre," 12. Cf. in Fr. Josef Bisig's brochure, 34–36, the motivations set out by Archbishop Lefebvre on 30 May 1988.
10   Fortunately, there are some priests and many faithful who attend SSPX chapels who do not share this attitude, and sometimes even deplore it.
11   Sometimes, however, leaders of the SSPX support on their own initiative what is commanded or advised by the hierarchy.

nullity of marriages internally. By this, the Society is clearly attributing to itself a power of jurisdiction.[12]

4. Fr. Gleize's definition of schism is incomplete. He restricts the concept of schism to the relationship with authority. "And if schism is defined as the claim of being able to give what the Pope alone can give, this power communicated by a consecration accomplished against the will of the Pope is schismatic."[13] However, does not Fr. Gleize here "falsify the most elementary data of Catholic doctrine," as he so kindly imagines we do? We rather think that, carried away by the needs of his argument, he has forgotten another dimension of schism: the attack on unity among the faithful.

"Those who refuse to submit to the Sovereign Pontiff and *those who refuse communion with the members of the Church who are subject to him are called schismatics,*" writes the Common Doctor.[14]

The SSPX openly asserts its separation from the other members of the Church. Fr. Pagliarani, in 2016, referred to "the objective fact that Catholic life within the official structures is currently impossible."[15] According to the directives of the superiors, one should not even attend the services of the *Ecclesia Dei* Institutes, or at least not receive

---

12   Since 1991, during Archbishop Lefebvre's lifetime, the SSPX has arrogated to itself over its faithful (and potentially over all Catholics), through the creation of the "St. Charles Borromeo Commission," the *power to bind and loose,* usurping the power of jurisdiction that only the Pope can give. In May 2017, eight deans of the SSPX District of France and three religious superiors affirmed, "We will continue to recognize only the St. Charles Borromeo Commission . . . as the ultimate judge of these [matrimonial] matters" (*Le Chardonnet,* n. 928, 4).

13   Gleize, "La Fraternité Saint Pierre," 11.

14   St. Thomas Aquinas, *ST* II-II, q. 39, a. 1. This definition was restated by the Code of Canon Law: CIC 1917, can. 1325 § 2; CIC 1983, can. 751.

15   Working document sent by Fr. Davide Pagliarani to Bishop Fellay, then Superior General, in preparation for a meeting of the Society's major superiors in Anzère in June 2016. The lecture that he gave on January 15, 2022 at the 15th Congress of the *Courrier de Rome* has the same tenor: https://laportelatine.org/formation/crise-eglise/garder-la-tradition-et-la-transmettre.

Holy Communion there. One must distance himself not only from the faithful who frequent the New Rite, but also from the "ralliés"[16] so as not to be contaminated by the "modernist" spirit that the latter are supposed to convey. Priests who are present at a religious ceremony of the "ralliés" must attend it outside the choir, and in any case without the choir habit (in a cassock without surplice). The faithful or priests who follow these directives are not behaving as members of the Church. The great theologian Cajetan may be invoked on this subject:

> He is schismatic who refuses to act as part of the Church. It does not matter what the reasons are: as soon as one refuses to act as part of the one Catholic Church, one falls into schism. However varied the reasons and passions may be that impel Christians to withdraw from communion, to want to sanctify and be sanctified, to instruct and be instructed, to lead and be led…, not as parts of the Catholic Church, but as if they were themselves separate "wholes," they are schismatics.[17]

These four reasons lead us to consider that our 1988 judgment remains entirely valid. Consecrations without a papal mandate (and *a fortiori* against the express will of the Pope) are not legitimate and constitute a very serious attack on the unity of the Church. Carried out with the intention of evading the jurisdiction of the Pope and the bishops, they constitute a "schismatic act." The fact that the group to which they have given rise refuses hierarchical communion (even after having received such positive offers) is a clear confirmation of this situation of deliberate separation.

Let us clarify an important point. We are aware of the dramatic situation of crisis in the Church. We see that many pastors are not performing their duty; some even

---

16   "Rallié" is a rather derogatory term used to designate a person who has joined a cause, after having been its opponent.

17   Cajetan, *Commentary on the Summa Theologiae*, II-II, q. 39, a. 1, n. 2.

give scandal in matters of faith and morals. We acknowledge that certain acts and omissions of the hierarchy favor heresy and the destruction of ecclesiastical structures. We understand that many of the rank-and-file faithful, being disoriented, cling to zealous priests who dispense the sacraments in their traditional form.[18] We are not here accusing persons. We are not saying that our confreres of the SSPX and their faithful, whose qualities we know, are all subjectively schismatic.

However, we have a duty as theologians to affirm fundamental theological truths. The text of Fr. Gleize gives us the opportunity to recall that one does not fight an error with another error, nor heresy with schism. We therefore do not share the pragmatic point of view of those who say to us: "Let's not make enemies among traditionalists—we want the traditional sacraments and catechesis, period!" This emphasis on efficiency can be seen as a traditionalist version of the "primacy of pastoral concerns." It is a short-term pragmatism that neglects the primacy of doctrine and distorts the minds of the faithful.

As priests, we have a duty to bear witness to the fact that, whatever the cost, we must remain faithful to all aspects of Catholic doctrine: the importance of Tradition, as well as that of hierarchical communion. As founders, we also see that this has been possible and that, in fact, by the grace of God, it has been fruitful.

---

18   The fact that Pope Francis, as of September 2015, conceded for the benefit of the faithful that those who confess to SSPX priests "will receive a valid absolution" does not mean that SSPX priests are in full communion with the Church. The Pope is perfectly able to grant powers to those who are separated, even if they do not ask for them, without meaning that he recognizes their full communion with the Catholic Church. According to many theologians, this is the case for the valid confessions of dissident Eastern Orthodox priests.

The Requirement of Rationality in Canonical Norms

ITS MEANING AND IMPLICATIONS, WITH PARTICULAR REFERENCE TO LITURGICAL LAW*

RÉGINALD-MARIE RIVOIRE, FSVF

"THE LAW IS NOTHING OTHER THAN an ordering of reason for the common good, promulgated by him who has care of the community."[1] This definition of St. Thomas Aquinas is admitted in theory by most canonists. And yet, rare are those who draw all of its conclusions when it comes concretely to elaborating or applying a law, and, more broadly, to determining what is just in a given situation.

If canon law has largely escaped from the theoretical positivism that characterizes secular law (which denies

---

* This conference was originally given in August 2023, at the *Speculum Iustitiae* Colloquium in La Crosse, Wisconsin. Fr. Réginald-Marie Rivoire, of the Fraternity of St. Vincent Ferrer, graduated from the *Institut d'Études Politiques* of Paris and holds a doctorate in canon law (Pontifical University of the Holy Cross, Rome). He is the Master of Studies of the students of the Friary of St. Thomas Aquinas in Chémeré-le-Roi, France, Defender of the Bond and Promotor of Justice at the ecclesiastical Tribunal of Rennes, France. He teaches canon law in various religious institutes.

1   St. Thomas Aquinas, *Summa Theologiae* [*ST*], I-II q. 90, a. 4, co.: "nihil est aliud quam quaedam rationis ordinatio ad bonum commune, ab eo qui curam communitatis habet, promulgata."

the existence of natural or divine law, or which sees at best a mere moral obligation provided that it not be recognized or protected by a positive norm), it is not exempt from a certain practical positivism, that which tends to consider that every norm emanating from authority possesses a binding character, independently even from its rationality.

This positivism has at times been variously qualified as "pious," "sacred," or "naive," for it bases itself apparently on good intentions such as Christian obedience to sacred pastors (cf. can. 212, §1), ecclesial communion (cf. can. 209), or even more the imperative for juridical security. It tends, however, to make the canonist into a mere acritical servant of the law, a technician of normative texts, and not a master of the Art of the Good and the Just (*ars boni et aequi*)—charged with saying the right (*ius-dicere*).

Faced with this practical positivism, the present article aims to recall the foundation of law and its limits, with particular attention to liturgical law. Among all ecclesial norms, this occupies a place apart. If liturgical norms have, without contest, a juridical dimension—inasmuch as they regulate and measure that which is just in the domain of the sacraments and worship—they are not for that matter merely disciplinary and contingent, liturgy being by nature a *protestatio fidei*—a profession of faith—and a constitutive element of holy and living Tradition.

Confronted with a voluntarist current, the First Part of this article will call to mind the essence of law and whence it draws its obligatory character. According to the Angelic Doctor, an irrational juridical norm, even if it is willed by the legislator and possesses all formal requisites, creates no juridical obligation for one to obey. The principles established by St. Thomas are valid analogically for every norm, including the canonical one. Even the Supreme Authority in the Church is not absolute.

The Second Part will strive to specify that which one understands by "rationality of a norm." Essentially, the

rationality of a norm is its adequation with the nature
of the things it purports to regulate. We will strive to
provide objective criteria enabling one to distinguish the
rational norm from the irrational. Not every defective
norm, in truth, is irrational.

Finally, the Third Part will describe the means apt to
guarantee the rationality of canonical norms.

I. THE ESSENCE OF LAW AND ITS OBLIGATORY CHARACTER

1.1 Terminological Precision: Ius, Norma *and* Lex

Etymologically, *"norma"* means the square, an instrument for measuring agricultural surfaces. The norm is a
rule, a measure. This fundamental meaning is found in all
uses of the word. Thus, in the moral domain, St. Thomas
defines a law (which in this case is indeed the equivalent
of a norm) as a rule and measure of acts, whereby man
is induced to act or is restrained from acting."[2]

In the juridical domain, the norm is the rule of law (*regula
iuris*), whereas St. Thomas tells us that the right is "the just
thing itself" (*ipsa res iusta*), the object of the virtue of justice,
which consists in giving each his own (*suum*).[3] It is important not to confuse the right and the norm. St. Thomas
explains that the norm is "not the right itself, but a certain
measure of the right,"[4] either in that the norm declares
a pre-existing right, or in that it indicates the conditions
required to constitute a right. One deduces from this that
the right is within things, while the norm is in the mind.

According to St. Thomas, it is from the right (*iustum*),
from the just thing, that the norm draws its legality, because

---

2   *ST*, I-II, q. 90, a. 1: "quædam regula et mensura actuum, secundum quam inducitur aliquis ad agendum, vel ab agendo retrahitur."
3   Cf. the famous definition of Ulpian, repeated in the *Digest*: "Justice
is the constant and perpetual will to render to each one his due."
"Iustitia est constans et perpetua voluntas ius suum cuique tribuendi"
(*Dig.* 1, 1, 10); cf. also *ST*, II-II, q. 58, a. 1.
4   *ST*, II-II, q. 57, a. 1, ad 2: "non est ipsum ius, proprie loquendo,
sed aliqualis ratio iuris."

the juridical is proper to the *ius*, to the right. Where there is no relationship of justice, there is no legal norm. This truth was expressed by the Roman jurist Paulus in the formula: "What is right is not derived from the rule but the rule arises from our knowledge of what is right."[5] A norm is not juridical because it deals with one matter rather than another, nor because it obeys a particular formalism, nor because trespassing it is punishable; it is legal in so far as it concerns rights.

It follows that, in and of itself, any subject capable of generating a right and of stating the consequences that flow from it for the future can be the author of a legal norm. It is not of the essence of the legal norm that it proceeds from a power superior to its addressees. There are many legal norms other than those which emanate from the public authority. Some, for example, are the result of private autonomy (contractual norms, statutes), while others originate from the community itself (customary norms).[6] All have this in common: they introduce a rule of just conduct.

It is true that, among juridical norms, a special place is occupied by those the purpose of which is to order social life with a view to the common good. Depending on whether these general norms originate from the authority in charge of the community or from the community itself, one will speak of either laws or customs. The law is therefore a written norm, of a general and abstract nature, which emanates from the public authority responsible for governing the community.

---

5   Dig. 50, 17, 1: "Non ex regula ius sumatur, sed ex iure quod est regula fiat."
6   To propose a necessary link between the juridical norm and the public power is not without major drawbacks. It does not permit a satisfactory account of certain normative phenomena of a juridical nature, such as contracts, international treaties, and statutes of association. It reduces a person's juridical autonomy to a pure concession from authority, by making all the legal effectiveness of human conduct dependent on the law. Fundamentally, it is the mark of a "normativistic" and positivist conception of law.

In this article, we will focus on laws, but what will be said about a law is certainly valid for all norms, including canonical ones. The latter only state the rules for just actions within the Church.

Among canonical norms, liturgical norms (whether formulated in the *Code*, or mainly in *extra-codicem* texts, such as the *Prænotanda* or the *Institutio generalis*, or even in the rubrics of liturgical books themselves) occupy a special place. They are juridical because they regulate a juridical good: public worship and the sacraments.[7] The faithful have the right to participate in liturgical worship according to the legitimately established order (cf. can. 214), and the Church has the right to enforce the legitimately established liturgy. Being juridical, liturgical norms are subject to the same substantive and formal requirements as other disciplinary norms. Notably, they must be rational.

1.2 Authority and Rationality

The law is an *ordinatio rationalis*, a "rational ordering."[8] A norm must be rational, as it is a "measuring"—a rule of just human conduct. In any order, it is the principle that regulates and measures all the rest, and the principle of activity is the end. The rule of activity can only be the right ordering to the end. And where there is ordering, there is an ordering intelligence. There is a reason that

7   Cf. Dominique Le Tourneau, *La dimension juridique du sacré* (Montréal: Wilson & Lafleur, 2012); Massimo Del Pozzo, *La giustizia nel culto. Profili giuridici della liturgia della Chiesa* (Rome: EDUSC, 2013); Carlos J. Errázuriz M., "La sacra liturgia, specie i sacramenti, quale bene giuridico ecclesiale," in G. Boni, E. Camassa, P. Canava, P. Lillo, V. Turchi (eds.), *Recte sapere. Studi in onore di Giuseppe Dalla Torre*, vol. I (Turin, 2014), 279-297.

8   The rational character of the law—well forgotten by modern legislators—has been the subject of abundant comment. Within the francophone sphere, essential are the works of Louis Lachance, O. P., *Le concept de droit selon Aristote et selon saint Thomas*, 2e éd. (Ottawa-Montréal: Éditions du Lévrier, 1948), ch. 3-6, 89-147; Michel Villey, *La formation de la pensée juridique moderne* (Paris: PUF, 2003), 149-201; Michel Bastit, *Naissance de la loi moderne. La pensée de la loi de saint Thomas à Suárez* (Paris: PUF, 1990), 23-168.

orders the means to the end. Fundamentally, law is an act of reason.

Admittedly, the will is taken into account in the genesis of the law: there would be no law passed if the legislator did not want it. However, because he wants a precise goal, his reason, set in motion by his will, determines and commands the appropriate means. If we cut it off from reason, the will is no more than a blind force. For St. Thomas, the famous formula of Ulpian—*Quod principi placuit, legis habet vigorem* ("what pleases the Prince has force of law")—can only be understood as the will of the Prince regulated by reason.[9] A law which is not rational, a law which comes solely from the goodwill of the Prince—or, in modern terms, solely from the "general will" of the citizens—could not be binding.

The binding nature of law therefore derives from its rationality, not from the power from which it emanates. For St. Thomas, the obligation does not consist in the will of the one who has authority. It is knowledge itself that is normative because it expresses the requirements of the real, of the good end to which we must strive, or— from a legal point of view—of the right (the good that is due) that we must recognize and respect. Intelligence is determined by known reality, and an act contrary to known reality is not a rational act. The law which is contrary to the reality which it claims to order does not

---

9　*Dig.* 1, 4, 1; cf. *ST*, I-II, q. 90, a. 1, ad 3: "Reason has its power of moving from the will, as stated above: for it is due to the fact that one wills the end, that the reason issues its commands as regards things ordained to the end. But in order that the volition of what is commanded may have the nature of law, it needs to be in accord with some rule of reason. And in this sense is to be understood the saying that the will of the sovereign has the force of law; otherwise, the sovereign's will would savor of lawlessness rather than of law."—"Ratio habet vim movendi a voluntate, ut supra dictum est, ex hoc enim quod aliquis vult finem, ratio imperat de his quæ sunt ad finem. Sed voluntas de his quæ imperantur, ad hoc quod legis rationem habeat, oportet quod sit aliqua ratione regulata. Et hoc modo intelligitur quod voluntas principis habet vigorem legis, alioquin voluntas principis magis esset iniquitas quam lex."

introduce an order, but a disorder. It is not a law, even if it has all the formal appearances. It does not oblige, not only morally, but even legally.

In the realist perspective, law is an act of reason which discovers an order, a relation of a means to an end. It is this order that it expresses in a command. Without this order, there is no law. The will intervenes, but only in a subordinate way. It is in fact indispensable to render effective the obligation that reason expresses, but in no way to create or ground this obligation. This seems obvious for laws that are only declarative of natural or positive divine law. But this is no less true of purely positive laws. Although the latter manifest a choice between different equally possible means, this choice of will is never purely arbitrary. It intervenes within a prudential process in which intellect and will constantly intersect, and whose main act, *imperium*, is substantially the work of reason.[10]

This essential link between the rationality of a law and its obligatory nature will be lost in modern times. A shift took place after Francisco Suárez († 1617), an author whose influence on canon law would be considerable. It is not possible to dwell long on this question: it would be the subject of another study. Let us simply note that for Suárez, the law is essentially an act of the will, a precept: "a law is a common precept, just and stable, sufficiently promulgated."[11]

---

10   Cf. *ST*, II-II, q. 47, a. 8: "Utrum præcipere sit principalis actus prudentiæ" and I-II, q. 17, a. 1: "Utrum præcipere sit actus rationis, seu voluntatis."

11   Francisco Suárez, *De Legibus ac Deo legislatore*, lib. I, cap. XII, n. 5: "Lex est commune præceptum, iustum ac stabile, sufficienter promulgatum." Suárez criticizes the Thomist definition in that, according to him, the criterion of rational ordering does not permit one truly to distinguish between the law and a mere exhortation or counsel. Before the intervention of the will, according to Suárez, there is no law. There is only an assertion, at most an exhortation. The difference between precepts and exhortations is precisely that the former are directives which the legislator has *willed* to impose, whereas the latter are directives which the legislator has *not* willed to impose. It is the will, and it alone, which obliges: it gives the force of law to that which would otherwise be only a simple assertion or

The law is an act of the superior who, by his will, binds the conscience of the subjects, because his authority derives from that of God. Suárez reduces the right to the law (this is known as normativism), and he degrades the law to the rank of a precept imposed by sovereign authority (this is voluntarism). One must obey the superior who commands: such is the first principle, according to Suárez.[12]

Who does not see the consequences of such a position? The will, necessarily attracted by the Good, remains indeterminate in relation to particular goods; it can adhere to any particular good, even if it is contrary to the common good. The unjust act, the arbitrary act, is not *rational*, but it remains *voluntary*. Of course, Suárez held that laws must be rational and that an unjust law is not a law.[13] Nevertheless, his position on the primacy of will was highly influential and paved the way for more extreme forms of voluntarism.[14] If the formal constituent of the law is in the will, the unjust, irrational law remains a law and must be obeyed. According to the voluntarist school of thought, the law obliges simply because it emanates from legitimate authority, regardless of whether it is just or not. The legislator certainly has the duty to legislate fairly, but it is a purely moral duty, without legal consequence. An

---

exhortation. St. Thomas would have responded that the difference between exhortations and precepts does not come from the will of the legislator to oblige or not, but from their very object, an object grasped by *reason* which consequently expresses a practical directive. While a precept concerns a work in itself necessary to attain an end, a mere exhortation concerns a work which is not in itself necessary to achieve that end. An exhortation therefore is not a sort of attenuated precept merely lacking the force of obligation imposed by authority.

12   Cf. *Ibid.*, lib. I, cap. XXVII, n. 7. Considered carefully, one cannot see how the principle "one must obey the superior who commands" can be the most fundamental. It is necessarily founded on the requirements of an order of things, imposed objectively. To obey God, one must recognize through reason that this must be so due to the creature's nature and that of the Creator. Therefore, there exists an objective order prior to the voluntary order, which gives the latter a rational basis.

13   Cf. *Ibid.*, lib. III, cap. III, n. 11.

14   See Michel Bastit, *Naissance de la loi moderne*, 307–333.

irrational law remains a law. Voluntarism, which bases the obligatory nature of law on the power of the legislator, necessarily results in positivism.

An example provided by the Jesuit Karl Rahner, undoubtedly a worthy son of Suárez, illustrates well this dissociation of law and morality. This passage is particularly appropriate, since it concerns liturgical law:

> Imagine that the Pope, as supreme pastor of the Church, issued a decree today requiring all the uniate churches of the Near East to give up their Oriental liturgy and adopt the Latin rite... The Pope would not exceed the competence of his jurisdictional primacy by such a decree; the decree would be legally valid. But we can also pose an entirely different question. Would it be morally licit for the Pope to issue such a decree? Any reasonable man and any true Christian would have to answer "no." Any confessor of the Pope would have to tell him that in the concrete situation of the Church today such a decree, despite its legal validity, would be subjectively and objectively an extremely grave moral offense against charity, against the unity of the Church rightly understood (which does not demand uniformity), against possible reunion of the Orthodox with the Roman Catholic Church, etc., a mortal sin from which the Pope could be absolved only if he revoked the decree.[15]

A Thomist would certainly respond to Rahner that such a "decree" would not merely be immoral, but illegal and invalid. An irrational decree cannot be legal.

1.3 The Limits of Authority in the Church

From this requirement of the rationality of norms flow the very limits of any legislative authority. The will of the legislator being normalized by reason—*ratione regulata*,

---

15   Karl Rahner, *Studies in Modern Theology* (Freiburg; London: Herder; Burns & Oates, 1965), 394–395.

writes St. Thomas—no authority on Earth is absolute. Legislative authority cannot make irrational laws because its power consists precisely in the faculty of ordering, while an irrational norm introduces disorder.

This certainly applies to authority in the Church, including the supreme authority. Of course, the Pope—by divine right—"possesses, in the Church, by virtue of his office, the ordinary, supreme, full, immediate and universal power which he can always freely exercise" (can. 331). However, as Professor Eduardo Baura recalls, commenting on an important speech of Benedict XVI at the Rota on January 21, 2012:

> [A]lthough power in the Church derives from divine and positive law, it is always a question of the capacity to fulfill a function (that, precisely, of ordering the life of the community towards its good), and not of a personal domination depending on the sole will of its owner. If ecclesiastical law obliges legally, that is to say establishes duties of justice, it is insofar as it constitutes rights (of the subjects or of the community itself) having as its title the order established for the community by him who is in charge of directing it so that it can achieve its good, and this order cannot be independent of the ordered reality. The claim to give legal value to the law for the reason that it emanates from the will of the legislator independently of the regulated reality... can only be based on legal positivism, even if it were "sacralized" by the consideration that ecclesiastical power derives from the divine foundation of the Church.[16]

The legislative power in the Church is not an unlimited power: it is the power to fulfill a social function, that is, to organize and regulate ecclesial life in order to lead it towards its good.

---

16   Eduardo Baura, "La realtà disciplinata quale criterio interpretativo giuridico della legge," *Ius Ecclesiæ* 24 (2012), 715.

Contrary to a widespread understanding according to which "the Pope can do anything," or that "what one Pope has done, another Pope can undo," it is necessary to recall that, in fact, the Pope cannot "do anything." Even in disciplinary matters, he is not an absolute monarch whose will is law. This is true, first of all, because he is obviously bound to respect divine law (the divine-apostolic tradition, which in part contains discipline); but also because he is not totally above certain human apostolic or ecclesiastical traditions, which maintain a more or less strong relationship of fittingness with the revealed deposit, for example, the discipline regarding priestly celibacy.

The liturgy is the privileged domain of this intertwining of the divine, the (simply) apostolic, and the ecclesiastical. Father Yves Congar remarked:

> We can see that there is often an entanglement of what is ecclesiastical with what is divine or apostolic—an entanglement such that, as clear (and important!) as the distinction is in principle, it cannot be pushed to the limit in real life. This situation favors a global respect; it even requires it. The critical spirit finds this difficult to deal with, but, while pursuing valid and even necessary distinctions, it must understand that, in the end, this relative indistinction in fact finds its explanation in the very nature of things. [17]

"This situation favors a global respect." Such respect is also, and even primarily, required of the Supreme Pontiff. Benedict XVI emphasized this in one of his first homilies (May 7, 2005):

> The pope is not an absolute monarch whose thoughts and desires are law. On the contrary: the pope's ministry is a guarantee of obedience to Christ and to his Word. He must not proclaim

---

[17] Yves Marie-Joseph Congar, O. P., *La Tradition et la vie de l'Église* (Paris: Fayard, 1963), 39-40.

> his own ideas, but rather constantly bind himself
> and the Church to obedience to God's Word, in
> the face of every attempt to adapt it or water it
> down, and every form of opportunism... The
> pope knows that in his important decisions, he is
> bound to the great community of faith of all times,
> to the binding interpretations that have developed
> throughout the Church's pilgrimage. Thus, his
> power is not being above, but at the service of, the
> Word of God. It is incumbent upon him to ensure
> that this Word continues to be present in its great-
> ness and to resound in its purity, so that it is not
> torn to pieces by continuous changes in usage.[18]

It is true that, in modern times, in the West, Popes
have appropriated the right to legislate in an ever more
detailed and extensive manner in liturgical matters. This
phenomenon increased even more in the twentieth century,
under the combined effect of a juridical positivism that was
very prevalent (even in the Church) and of an ecclesiology
that tended to absolutize the power of the Pope. So much
so that, as noted by Joseph Ratzinger, "after the Second
Vatican Council, the impression arose that the pope really
could do anything in liturgical matters, especially if he
were acting on the mandate of an ecumenical council."[19]

In fact, we have just seen that Karl Rahner envisaged
seriously that a Pope could validly suppress all the Oriental rites!

Yet the power of the Pope is at the service of the
Church's holy and living Tradition, which he must always
preserve and pass down. This is especially true in relation
to the liturgy, which is one of the constitutive elements
of that Tradition. Cardinal Ratzinger once explained this
using the striking image of a gardener in his garden,
as opposed to a technician who makes machines: "with

---

18   Pope Benedict XVI, "Homily at Mass of Possession of the
Chair of the Bishop of Rome," May 7, 2005, in *AAS* 97 (2005), 748-752
19   Joseph Ratzinger, *Spirit of the Liturgy*, Commemorative Edition
(San Francisco: Ignatius Press, 2018), 179-80.

respect to the liturgy, [the Pope] has the task of a gardener, not that of a technician who builds new machines and throws the old ones on the junk pile."[20]

The same is summarized in the *Catechism of the Catholic Church*, n. 1125: "Even the supreme authority in the Church may not change the liturgy arbitrarily, but only in the obedience of faith and with religious respect for the mystery of the liturgy."

Given the above, one understands that a pontifical liturgical law which does not respect the very nature of the liturgy would not be a law, a *regula iuris*, but rather a *corruptela iuris*, a "corruption of the law," even if it were guaranteed by all juridical forms. It would lack that fundamental character of any law, which is rationality. Since the act of law-making is an act of reason, it is itself conditioned, governed by the nature of things.

2. THE RATIONALITY OF THE NORM

What makes a norm rational, and what makes it not?

2.1 Characteristics of the Rational Norm

The rationality of norms should not be understood as a purely formal, logical or grammatical rationality. A norm is not merely a logical proposition; it is an *ordinatio*, that is, it is an act of reason which arranges elements with a view to an end, taking into account the nature of those elements. The rationality of a norm therefore designates its dependence and its adequacy to the objective reality that it claims to order: its realism.

Javier Hervada, the famous professor at the University of Navarre, gives three conditions for a legal norm to be rational: it must be adequate to human nature, the common good, and social circumstances.[21] These conditions apply

---

20   Preface to *The Organic Development of the Liturgy* by Alcuin Reid, OSB (San Francisco: Ignatius Press, 2005).
21   Javier Hervada, *Lecciones Propedéuticas de Filosofía del Derecho*, 3rd ed. (Pamplona: EUNSA, 2000), 357.

mutatis mutandis to Church norms. An essential characteristic of their rationality will be their adequacy to the nature of the Church. Thus, a liturgical law cannot contradict the essence of a sacrament, the role of sacred ministers, etc.

This rationality of a norm is a practical rationality. The law is "something of reason," but of practical reason, not of speculative reason; reason measuring action, not reason measured by its object. An important consequence follows: a law is not the fruit of speculative reasoning which relates to universal and necessary beings, but of practical and prudential reasoning which includes a contingent element. There is not just one law possible to achieve this or that end, and it would be absurd to demand of human laws the "infallibility" enjoyed by the demonstrative conclusions of the sciences.[22] A law is inherently contingent, changing, dependent on circumstances.

This contingency of the object explains why the power of government, even the supreme government in the

---

22   Cf. St. Thomas Aquinas, *ST*, I-II, q. 91, a. 3, ad 3: "The practical reason is concerned with practical matters, which are singular and contingent: but not with necessary things, with which the speculative reason is concerned. Wherefore human laws cannot have that inerrancy that belongs to the demonstrated conclusions of sciences. Nor is it necessary for every measure to be altogether unerring and certain, but according as it is possible in its own particular genus."— "Ratio practica est circa operabilia, quæ sunt singularia et contingentia, non autem circa necessaria, sicut ratio speculativa. Et ideo leges humanæ non possunt illam infallibilitatem habere quam habent conclusiones demonstrativæ scientiarum. Nec oportet quod omnis mensura sit omni modo infallibilis et certa, sed secundum quod est possibile in genere suo"; *ST*, I-II, q. 94, a. 4: "The practical reason, on the other hand, is busied with contingent matters, about which human actions are concerned: and consequently, although there is necessity in the general principles, the more we descend to matters of detail, the more frequently we encounter defects... But in matters of action, truth or practical rectitude is not the same for all, as to matters of detail, but only as to the general principles..."— "Sed ratio practica negotiatur circa contingentia, in quibus sunt operationes humanæ: et ideo, etsi in communibus sit aliqua necessitas, quanto magis ad propria descenditur, tanto magis invenitur defectus... In operativis autem non est eadem veritas vel rectitudo practica apud omnes quantum ad propria, sed solum quantum ad communia..."

Church, does not enjoy the infallibility that the power of the magisterium enjoys under certain very specific conditions. A doctrinal statement is true or false and, under certain conditions, it can be guaranteed from error by infallible assistance. A law will always be more or less prudent. There is no prudential infallibility. When it comes to the power of jurisdiction, there can be no question of infallibility in the proper sense: divine assistance is always relative, even when the measures taken are of universal scope. Failures, recklessness, and even abuse of authority are always possible.

However, it is not every imperfection that makes a law irrational. A norm is not irrational simply because it is defective, questionable, or insufficient, but only if it introduces disorder, because it is contrary to the nature of things, to the common ecclesial good, or because it is impossible to apply without harmful results.

We will understand this better by examining some characteristics of an irrational norm.

2.2 Characteristics of the Irrational Norm

A recent highly controversial liturgical law will provide us with many examples of irrational normative provisions. I refer, as some may have divined, to the motu proprio *Traditionis custodes.*

According to J. Hervada,[23] a norm is irrational: 1) when it is immoral or unjust (contrary to natural or positive divine law); 2) when it is so inadequate to social reality that it introduces disorder and not order; or 3) when it is technically impossible to apply: it is then a "stupid" norm which is intrinsically contradictory.

a) First of all, a law is irrational if it contradicts in its statement the very reality that it claims to order. A legislative statement can indeed quite simply deny reality. As I have already pointed out in my book:

---

23   Javier Hervada, *Lecciones Propedéuticas de Filosofía del Derecho*, 364–365.

The provision of *TC* that has caused the most astonishment and has already attracted much attention is undoubtedly article 1, whereby the pope decides that "the liturgical books promulgated by Saint Paul VI and Saint John Paul II, in conformity with the decrees of Vatican Council II, are the unique expression of the *lex orandi* of the Roman Rite."

Concise as it is, this article is the exact opposite of article 1 of the motu proprio *Summorum pontificum*, which stated:

> "The Roman Missal promulgated by Pope Paul VI is the Ordinary expression of the *lex orandi* of the Catholic Church of the Latin rite. The Roman Missal promulgated by Saint Pius V and revised by Blessed John XXIII is nonetheless to be considered an extraordinary expression of the same *lex orandi* of the Church and duly honored for its venerable and ancient usage. These two expressions of the Church's *lex orandi* will in no way lead to a division in the Church's *lex credendi*; for they are two usages of the one Roman Rite."

We find here a truly striking contrast between two manners of legislating, one marked by juridical realism, the other by voluntaristic positivism. Whilst Benedict XVI acknowledged, by a declarative act, two ritual realities which, *de facto*, exist today in the Latin Church (one dating back to antiquity, the other to 1969), and sought to give them a juridical framework, Francis decides, by a performative act, that only one of these two realities exists in the Church, in this case the one born in 1969; the other no longer exists. It already no longer exists in law, and the legislator wills that it disappear in fact.

In article 1 of *Summorum pontificum*, the normative act is a rational one, not primarily because it is the fruit of the legislator's reasoning, but because it is measured by an objective reality that imposes itself on the legislator (indeed, reality itself does not come under his *dominium*): there are two ritual realities and the legislator intends to order them in the best way possible in view of the common good, giving them a juridical name (ordinary or extraordinary "form" of the Roman Rite), and a corresponding juridical regime. One might discuss the choice of this innovative terminology and the juridical régime attached thereto, but one cannot deny that the pope has exercised legislative prudence. In article 1 of *TC*, on the other hand, the normative act, certainly preceded—one would hope—by reasoning, appears more as an act of the will of the legislator. The logic followed is normativistic and legalistic, which is not only inappropriate in itself, but seems particularly unsuited to the field of liturgy, which it claims to regulate: a Roman Missal is not the highway code. Contradicting one's predecessor would have been less shocking than treating a liturgical rite as a merely disciplinary matter.[24]

Let us note that what article 1 of *TC* states is in contradiction, on the one hand, with the current existence of other expressions of the *lex orandi* of the Roman Rite which are by no means destined to disappear, such as the Zairian form and the form of the Anglican Ordinariate (*Divine Worship*), and, on the other hand, with article 93 of the Apostolic Constitution *Praedicate Evangelium* of March 19, 2023 (therefore, post-*TC*) reforming the Roman Curia:

> The Dicastery [for Divine Worship] is concerned with the regulation and discipline of the sacred liturgy with regard to the use—granted according to established norms—of liturgical books prior to the reform of the Second Vatican Council.

---

24   Réginald-Marie Rivoire, *Does* Traditionis Custodes *Pass the Juridical Rationality Test?* (Lincoln, NE: Os Justi Press, 2022), 118.

Thus, a very solemn document confirms the perennial nature of the traditional liturgy, since it admits the possibility of using the liturgical books prior to the reform, even though they would no longer be (according to article 1 of *TC*) an expression of the *lex orandi* of the Latin Rite. Let him understand who can...

b) A norm which does not respect "that which essentially constitutes juridical institutes" (cf. can. 86).

Imagine, for example, a bishop who would like to erect a parish in which none of the sacraments would be offered to the well-disposed faithful. This would go against the very nature of a parish. The establishment of a parish always entails the exercise, guaranteed to the faithful, of full pastoral care (*cura pastoralis*; cf. can. 515 §1). Although a bishop may, for a just cause, suppress an already erected parish (cf. can. 515 §2), he may not create the juridical monster that would be a parish without Mass or without sacraments. This would be like trying to square a circle.

This is not a figment of the imagination. It is what the Cardinal Vicar of Rome decided in a "Pastoral Letter" dated October 7, 2021, Prot. n. 1845/21: "Every day, except for the Easter Triduum, the faithful will be able to participate in the Eucharistic celebration according to the *Missale Romanum* of 1962 in the Santissima Trinità dei Pellegrini Parish (cf. art. 3 §5, *Traditionis custodes*)." During the three holiest days of the liturgical year, therefore, the faithful of this personal parish are expected to go elsewhere to seek the salvific goods. Such a provision is invalid, because it goes against the very nature of a parish. In fact, a few months later, it was revoked.

c) A law that is impossible to enforce. Since a law is a general standard, established for the majority of cases, it should be able to apply in the majority of cases. The fact that an authority must dispense from it in the majority of cases is a sure sign that the law is irrational, because it is inapplicable.

For example, immediately after the publication of *Traditionis custodes*, it was clear that article 3 §2, which forbids public celebrations according to the *usus antiquior* in parish churches, is inapplicable in many countries where there are almost exclusively parish churches. Many diocesan bishops—before the *Responsa* were published—had to dispense from this provision under canon 87 §1. Others made no formal decision, letting Masses take place in an apparent illegality, in keeping with the axiom *ad impossibilia nemo tenetur* ("no one is bound to do the impossible"). This is a good example of the non-acceptance of an irrational legislative provision.

d) Norms that do not respect the principle of legality or the hierarchy of norms.

In administrative canon law, the principle of legality means, simply put, that ecclesiastical authority is subject to the law. Ecclesiastical administration must exercise its powers within its own limits and with due regard for the norms that have been legitimately established.

A lower norm that contradicts a higher norm is irrational. The *Responsa ad Dubia* of the Dicastery for Divine Worship offer us many examples of this which I list in my book.[25]

According to the principle of the hierarchy of norms, "a lower legislator cannot validly issue a law contrary to higher law" (can. 135, §2). Thus, a bishop can legislate for the liturgy within his diocese, but he cannot narrow the options that the universal law permits. Unfortunately, that is exactly what many bishops did during the pandemic, when they forbade communion on the tongue, whereas it is, according to universal law, always a right of the faithful.[26]

I would also like to mention as an example the so-called "Policy for the archdiocese of Chicago for implementing

---

25   Cf. R.-M. Rivoire, *Does* Traditionis Custodes *Pass the Juridical Rationality Test?*, 76–78.
26   Cf. R.-M. Rivoire, "La situation juridique de la communion dans la main," in *Bref examen critique de la communion dans la main*, Preface by Cardinal Raymond Burke (Versailles: Contretemps, 2021), 97–113.

Traditionis Custodes," dated December 25, 2021.[27] Article 6 of this Policy states:

> Priests and those groups that receive permission from the Archbishop of Chicago to celebrate the Mass using the Missal of 1962, are bound on the first Sunday of the month to celebrate Mass only using the Missal of Paul VI. If Latin is used, then the faithful should be provided the means to participate in the responses. Mass is also ordinarily to be celebrated *versus populum*, unless permission is granted otherwise by the Archbishop. Additionally, all celebrations of the Church's liturgies on Christmas, the Triduum, Easter Sunday, and Pentecost Sunday are to use exclusively the liturgical books promulgated by Saint Pope Paul VI and Saint Pope John Paul II, either in the vernacular or in Latin, and ordinarily *versus populum*, unless permission is granted otherwise by the bishop. The intention of these requirements is to foster and make manifest the unity of this local Church, as well as to provide all Catholics in the Archdiocese an opportunity to offer a concrete manifestation of the acceptance of the teaching of the Second Vatican Council and its liturgical books.

Apart from the fact that *nowhere* did the Council envisage the celebration of Mass facing the people, this measure forbidding the celebration *ad orientem* is illegal and invalid, because the current *General Instruction of the Roman Missal* does not prescribe that the priest face toward the congregation or in the same direction as the congregation: it remains optional in the new rite of the Mass, and therefore a priest has always the right to celebrate *ad orientem*.

We could multiply the examples. Let us think of the

---

27   The text of the Policy was published in the newspaper of the archdiocese of Chicago, *Chicago Catholic*, Wednesday, January 5, 2022, available online: https://www.chicagocatholic.com/chicagoland/-/article/2022/01/05/archdiocese-sets-policy-for-implementing-traditionis-custodes-

norms which do not respect the just autonomy of inferior realities (in particular, which do not respect the "patrimony"—in the sense of canon 578—of religious institutes and their own right).[28]

Such normative provisions are not simply confused, defective, questionable, and inappropriate. They are truly and properly irrational and, consequently, are deprived of all legal value and entail no obligation to obey, even if they have all the formal appearances of a law and even if their non-observance is liable to sanctions from authority. In this case, the sanctions will only be *vis et iniuria*. St. Thomas is very clear on this point: "Human law has the nature of law in so far as it partakes of right reason.... But in so far as it deviates from reason, it is called an unjust law, and has the nature, not of law but of violence (*non habet rationem legis, sed magis violentiae*)."[29]

2.3 The Presumption of Rationality and Juridical Security

This doctrine of St. Thomas on the irrational law, *magis iniquitas quam lex* ("rather iniquity than law"), may seem too radical to positivist minds. Doesn't it risk undermining legal certainty and inciting disobedience towards sacred pastors? Isn't any subject going to evade an ecclesial norm by invoking its irrationality?

---

28   See Louis-Marie de Blignières, "The Pope and the Law of Religious Institutes," in *Sedes Sapientiae*, Special English-Language Issue (2022): 15–19. Such patrimony is to be faithfully maintained by all, including the hierarchy (can. 578: "ab omnibus fideliter servanda sunt"). Contrary to a widespread positivistic opinion, it is not in fact correct to affirm, without further qualification, that the pope may change the Constitutions approved by him. "In the event of deviations or abuses, a Commissioner may be appointed, but he must always govern *according to the proper law* of the institute (Rule, Constitutions, Directory ...). If circumstances are such that some of the means previously employed are no longer feasible or are no longer effective for obtaining the proper purpose of the institute, the hierarchy may, for those reasons, make changes to the Constitutions." Fr. de Blignières goes on to note that the hierarchy can also, in very serious and rare cases, suppress the Institute; yet it cannot change its essential patrimony and its purpose.

29   *ST*, I-II, q. 93, a. 3, ad 2.

Professors Hervada and Baura observe, however, that security must be, precisely, "juridical," that is, at the service of a *just* order. What would be the use of security that would guarantee the application of irrational and unjust norms? The famous words of the Prussian jurist Ihering: "Better an injustice than disorder," are the watchwords of positivism; for a realist jurist, however, they are inherently contradictory, for an injustice will always *in itself* be a disorder.

In fact, legal realism offers much more security than positivism, because it is the confrontation with reality. The real always offers more security than a text, which is susceptible to various interpretations and always easy to manipulate.

In addition, there is a presumption of rationality of a norm established by a competent authority according to the required formalities. It is up to the subject who claims that a norm is irrational to prove it and to resort to all the legal means at his disposal to do so.

The fact remains that, when St. Thomas says that there is no obligation to obey a manifestly unjust law, this implies that subjects can notice that a law is unjust, since no superior is going to say: "This law I'm promulgating is unjust." Naturally, subjects must be careful to exercise this right only with prudence and the fear of God. The rationality we are talking about has nothing to do with a subjectivist rationalism, let alone with sentimentalism. An unjust norm is a *concrete* reality, objectively noticeable.

An irrational, unjust law does not oblige. There is no moral duty to obey an unjust law, except *per accidens*, exceptionally, when material "disobedience"[30] risks causing greater evils (scandal) or in order to perform an act of virtue (humility, charity). However, the fundamental principle that "disorder does not order" still remains valid.

---

30   Strictly speaking, one should not speak of "disobedience" in such a case, because the norm simply does not oblige and therefore there is no matter for obedience.

3. THE MEANS FOR ENSURING THE RATIONALITY OF CANONICAL NORMS

By way of a conclusion, I would like to recall some means of guaranteeing the rationality of canonical norms. A priori, there is an art of rationally elaborating norms; a posteriori, an art of rationally applying previously established norms. We will content ourselves with giving a few examples, which are obviously not exhaustive.

3.1 The Art of Legislating Rationally

We have defined the rationality of a law as its adequacy to the social reality that it claims to order. It is therefore necessary in the first place that the legislator has a fair knowledge of this reality. This is especially true when the reality in question is the liturgy. A legislator who has a poor knowledge of the liturgy, in particular of what a rite is, will never be able to legislate correctly. I have shown elsewhere how the following is true:

> A liturgical rite is more than a thousand-year-old custom: considered in its integrity, it is a true Apostolic Tradition. For this reason, it is a juridically unavailable reality. It cannot be prohibited. "Such rites can die, if those who have used them in a particular era should disappear, or if the life situation of those same people should change. The authority of the Church has the power to define and limit the use of such rites in different historical situations, but she never just purely and simply forbids them!"[31]

In addition to knowing the reality on which he intends to legislate, part of the aptitude of the legislator is the fact of finding the clearest formulae for legislative texts.

---

31   Cf. R.-M. Rivoire, *Does* Traditionis Custodes *pass the Juridical Rationality Test?*, 60. Quotation from Joseph Ratzinger, "Ten Years of the Motu Proprio *Ecclesia Dei*," a lecture given by Cardinal Ratzinger at the Ergife Palace Hotel, Rome on Saturday October 24, 1998, *Adoremus Bulletin* (December 31, 2007), https://adoremus.org/2007/12/ten-years-of-the-motu-proprio-quotecclesia-deiquot/.

However, the clarity of a norm is not limited to its literal content. Its normative value, its rank, its effectiveness in derogating from other norms, its application to past situations etc., must also appear clearly.

From that point of view, we can only deplore the side-lining, during the present pontificate, of the Pontifical Council for Legislative Texts—the Dicastery specially in charge of providing technical and juridical expertise to the Supreme Pontiff and the Roman Curia in the elaboration of universal norms.[32] At the diocesan level, this work of expertise is normally carried out by the chancellor, who advises the bishop and also affixes his signature to the norms that the latter promulgates.

A very important point is also the identification of the author of the norm. Is it the Roman Pontiff or the Dicastery? If the norms are of an administrative nature, they cannot derogate from laws and have no value as soon as they oppose them (can. 33 § 1). If the Dicastery claims to act in legislative matters by delegation of the Roman Pontiff, the recipients of the norms must know the terms of the delegation and be able to verify that the administrative authority has acted within the limits of the mandate granted. However, the Dicastery often limits itself to inserting at the end of the document a formula such as *vigore facultatum a Summo Pontifice tributarum*, or *de speciali mandato Summi Pontificis*, but does not provide information on the content of these special faculties.

Even less can a Dicastery content itself with inserting a formula such as this: "The Supreme Pontiff Francis, in the course of an Audience granted to the Prefect of this Congregation on 18 November 2021, was informed of and gave his consent to the publication of these *Responsa ad dubia* with attached *Explanatory notes*."

---

32   See Geraldina Boni, *La recente attività normativa ecclesiale: finis terræ per lo ius canonicum? Per una valorizzazione del ruolo del Pontificio Consiglio per i testi legislativi e della scienza giuridica nella Chiesa* (Modena: Mucchi Editore, 2021).

On this point, it is very regrettable that the *General Regulations of the Roman Curia* (RGCR) are rarely followed, especially with regard to the necessary approval *in forma specifica* by the Roman Pontiff of provisions *contra legem* (RGCR, art. 126).

Finally, we cannot place too much importance on promulgation, which must be done in a clear manner. Promulgation is too often confused with a simple disclosure, whereas it is the publication of the authentic text attached to the *intimatio*. Promulgation is also part of the essence of a law, and without an authentic publication giving binding force to its text, a law does not exist (cf. can. 7: "Lex instituitur cum promulgatur"). An uncertain promulgation is equivalent to an uncertain law from its beginning. It seriously infringes the rights of the recipients of the law.

3.2 The Art of Applying Norms Rationally

Much remains that could be said here. The application of a canonical norm naturally depends a great deal on the concept that one has of the norm itself. Here again, Eduardo Baura gives us valuable hints.[33]

If a norm is conceived as an order in the sense of *iussum*, of command, which obliges because it emanates from the competent authority, the addressee (and the interpreter) will have to seek above all what is the will of the legislator. This, even if it is arbitrary, will always be binding. For example, the "decree" of 11 February 2022 by which Pope Francis recognizes that the FSSP is not affected by the new norms (both *TC* and the *Responsa ad dubia*, two months prior to the decree), will be seen as a pure *fait du prince* (arbitrary government act), easily revocable.[34]

---

33   Cf. Eduardo Baura, "Il sistema normativo liturgico. Tipologia e natura dei provvedimenti regolativi del culto," in *Diritto e norma nella liturgia*, ed. E. Baura and M. Del Pozzo (Milano: Giuffrè, 2016), 250–52.
34   The text of this decree can be found on the F. S. S. P. website: https://fssp.com/decree/.

If one considers that a norm is only the text, because it is the only objective empirical datum, then one would be satisfied with a textual interpretation. We would thus fall into a very positivist formalism, for which only the grammatical or logical meaning of the text counts. For example, we could conduct an exegesis of the decree of 11 February 2022 line by line, and we could emphasize that it concerns only the FSSP.

On the contrary, if one starts from a realistic conception of the law, conceived as the rational order established by the legislator in order to direct society towards its good, then what matters is to seek the precise order established, which depends on ordered reality. Ordered reality is the determining criterion of interpretation. The law is not merely a text. The formulation of the rule is not enough to know the ordered reality.

From this viewpoint, the decree appears as a full recognition of the proper right of the FSSP. It is therefore difficult to see how this recognition would not also apply to the institutes that share the same nature, that is, to all those that formerly depended on the Pontifical Commission *Ecclesia Dei*. The permanence of the special faculties granted is guaranteed by the proper law of the institute, which has received definitive approval. Granted in 1988 and recognized again in 2022, these special but habitual faculties are an integral element of the juridical status of these institutes and, as such, are perpetual.

In conclusion, Canon Law is certainly not devoid of technical instruments making it possible to guarantee a minimum of rationality of norms. But we still have to use these instruments. They will remain ineffective if there is not first a radical change of mentality among the lawmakers. Rediscovering the sense of legal realism of St. Thomas, by fighting against voluntarism, normativism, and positivism, seems to me to be the most urgent task of canonists today.

SELECTED BIBLIOGRAPHY

Baura, Eduardo. *Parte generale del diritto canonico. Diritto e sistema normativo*. Rome: EDUSC, 2013.

——. "Profili giuridici dell'arte di legiferare nella Chiesa," *Ius Ecclesiæ* 19 (2007): 13–36.

——. "Norma canónica." In *Diccionario General de Derecho Canónico*, vol. 5, edited by J. Otaduy, A. Viana, and J. Sedano (Cizur Menor: Aranzadi, 2012). 570–575.

——. "La realtà disciplinata quale criterio interpretativo giuridico della legge," *Ius Ecclesiæ* 24 (2012): 705–717.

——. "Il sistema normativo liturgico. Tipologia e natura dei provvedimenti regolativi del culto." In *Diritto e norma nella liturgia*, edited by E. Baura and M. Del Pozzo (Milano: Giuffrè, 2016). 218–252.

——. "La razionalità ovverossia il realismo della legge canonica." In *Sacrorum canonum scientia. Radici, tradizioni, prospettive. Studi in onore del Cardinale Péter Erdö per il suo 70° compleanno*, edited by Péter Szabó and Tamás Frankó (Budapest: Szent István Társulat, 2022). 78–91.

Hervada, Javier. *Lecciones Propedéuticas de Filosofía del Derecho*, 3rd ed. (Pamplona: EUNSA, 2000). 355–372.

Otaduy, Javier. "Ratio canonica." In *Diccionario General de Derecho Canónico*, vol. 6, edited by J. Otaduy, A. Viana, and J. Sedano (Cizur Menor: Aranzadi, 2012). 698–704.

——. "La *ratio* en las fuentes normativas del derecho canónico," *Ius canonicum* 49 (2009): 149–194.

Rivoire, Réginald-Marie. *Does* Traditionis Custodes *Pass the Juridical Rationality Test?* (Lincoln, NE: Os Justi Press, 2022).

Schouppe, Jean-Pierre. "Positivismo, normativismo e realismo giuridico nello *ius Ecclesiæ*," *Ius Ecclesiæ* 33 (2021): 569–593.

The Re-Formation of Thomists

A DEBATE ON
THE SINS OF ANGELS

AIDAN NICHOLS, O.P.

I N RECENT YEARS THE COUVENT SAINT-
Thomas-d'Aquin at Chémeré-le-Roi has been discussing the sins of angels. If to Anglo-Saxon ears this
report sounds comical, it is because many anglophone
Catholics, even if theologically educated, are unaware that
some of Thomas' most sophisticated analyses of the interplay of intelligence and love are to be found in the lengthy
section of the *Summa theologiae* devoted to the angelic creatures. Indeed, it could truly be said that Thomas treated
the angelic world not only for its own sake but also as a
philosophical and theological workshop in which to refine
his understanding of our own spiritual powers. Needless to
say, Thomas' corpus extends well beyond this most famous
of his writings, not just to the other less theologically
ambitious *Summa contra Gentiles* and to his biblical com-
mentaries—now taken with increasing seriousness, both
for their own value and for their contribution to a grasp
of his mind. Additionally, his works of the kind known
as "Disputed Questions" will often turn out to be the best
place to look for especially probing and fruitful discussions
of difficult points. This generalization about Thomas' work
is thoroughly well known to the Thomists of France, who
remain outstanding representatives of the tradition of the
Angelic Doctor in the twentieth and twenty-first centuries,
even if the Americans are rapidly catching up.

A major theological inspiration of the Fraternity of
St. Vincent Ferrer was the eminent Dominican mathe-
matician and metaphysician Michel-Louis Guérard des
Lauriers who, at a crucial point in the mid-twentieth
century debate about the relation between the natural
and the supernatural economies, brought his sabre-sharp
mind to bear on the significantly divisive question of the
origin of angelic sin.[1] The question was not *simply* divisive,
as might be—for those wishing to acquire the mind of
St. Thomas—any problematic topic where the texts of
Aquinas point in different directions. It was *significantly*
divisive, because from this particular *crux*, or knotty point,
in Thomasian interpretation, potentially enormous dif-
ferences open up in the overall assessment of Thomas'
philosophical and theological vision.

According to the essay on this subject by Joseph-Marie
Gilliot,[2] it was Guérard des Lauriers' achievement to have
proposed for this topic an adjudication which is not only
historically and speculatively satisfying (that is, historically plausible and speculatively coherent), but one which
throws open the Thomist school to an augmentation of
perspectives on an issue—the uniqueness of persons—
where its resources have been, in previous generations,
unduly limited. It is owing, first and foremost, to the
perceived limitation of those resources that the Personalist
movement in modern Catholicism was able, in the course
of the twentieth century, to challenge successfully the
predominance of Thomist thought, at the expense, unfortunately, of the wider range of constructive metaphysics

---

1   Michel-Louis Guérard des Lauriers, O. P., *Le Péché et la durée de
l'ange* (Rome-Parigi-Tournai-New-York: Desclée & Cie, 1965); see
also the same author's review of Charles Journet, Jacques Maritain,
Philippe de la Trinité, *Le péché de l'Ange. Peccabilité, nature et surnature*
(Paris: Beauchesne, 1961) in *Angelicum* 40 (1963): 202–214.
2   Joseph-Marie Gilliot, "La structure du libre arbitre et le péché
de l'ange. L'apport de Guérard des Lauriers à un débat du XXe siècle,"
Revue des sciences philosophiques et théologiques 104 (2020): 523–549. This study
published in the journal of the Dominicans of the Province of France
looks back to conversations at Chémeré-le-Roi in the previous year.

which both philosophy and dogmatic theology, in their different ways, require.[3] So, if Guérard des Lauriers is correct in his 1965 work *Le Péché et la durée de l'ange*, not only is the consistency—on a single controverted issue—of Thomas' corpus assured, but one particular perspective on the overall interpretation of his writing is commended, and the strong possibility emerges of an extension and strengthening of the Thomist tradition in a vital area (that of *persons*, in their uniqueness) where, not unreasonably, it has been taxed by critics with narrowness and weakness.

So far as the remote origins of this promising (largely future) development are concerned, the question at issue is relatively easy to state. Does the structure of angelic psychology—the purity and incisiveness of an angel's intellectual appetite, enjoyed from the beginning of its existence—guarantee an indefectible hold on its own commensurate good, such that only a dramatic transition of the angelic creature from the natural to the supernatural order could introduce a hiatus where aversion from God might occur? (A) Or, contrariwise, is it the case that, as with any other created possessor of freedom, an angel must be accounted naturally fallible in its own proper choices? (B) Let us call these "Position A" and "Position B."

In the *Disputed Questions on Evil*, Thomas aligns himself with the "dramatic transition" thesis of Position A. In Gilliot's words, "this summons to a destiny that goes beyond the angel's nature grounds the possibility of sin: the angel

---

3   In 1946, the publication of Henri de Lubac's *Surnaturel*, drawing support from texts of Thomas Aquinas, had called into question the thesis of the angel's natural impeccability, until then (almost) unanimously accepted in the Thomist School. The debate then became polarized along the lines of two readings of Aquinas. The reason for the angel's sinfulness is to be sought either in his elevation to the supernatural order (*De malo*, q. 16, a. 4), or in the very structure of the angelic creature (*Summa theologiae*, I, q. 63, a. 1). Guérard establishes that the foundation of spiritual creatures' freedom—and thus their peccability—lies at the heart of their metaphysical constitution, in the real distinction between nature and person, without necessarily involving the distinction between the natural and supernatural orders.

must make a choice for or against God."[4] Guérard terms
this element in Position A the "argument from order,"
since it turns on the distinction between the natural and
supernatural realms.

Does that then entail that, for Thomas, the angel is
unconditionally impeccable within the order of nature,
thus ratifying the "indefectible hold on its own commensurate good" element in Position A and thereby entirely
excluding Position B? For Guérard this is not the case.
Slippage from acceptance of the "dramatic transition" to
acceptance of the "indefectible hold" results from a failure to distinguish two "moments" within the "beginning"
of the angel's existence to which a more careful reading
of the *Summa theologiae* discussion should have alerted
Thomas' readers.

The "beginning" comprises, in the first place, the
moment when divine creative agency confers, with
the fundamental being of the angel, the activation of
all within the angel which belongs to its nature as, in
the real economy of creation, God envisages it. Here, in
Guérard's words, the "angel's operation is immediately
under the divine creative motion" which, as sheer divine
agency, must be indefectible, thereby excluding failure in
attaining the angel's true good: namely, sin.[5] And this
is so without any reference to the distinction between
the natural and supernatural orders, a statement which
Guérard feels confident making since, in his judgment,
the question of a hypothetical order of pure nature, a
"purely ideal and non-existent order to which by definition
[the angel] remains forever alien,"[6] simply does not arise
in the *Summa theologiae*. That question only arises, for

---

4   *Ibid.*, 529.
5   M.-L. Guérard des Lauriers, *Le Péché et la durée de l'ange*, 89: "Il est
en droit impossible que l'Ange pèche au premier instant parce qu'en
fait en cet instant l'opération de l'Ange est immédiatement sous la
motion divine créatrice."
6   Jacques Maritain, "Le péché de l'ange. Essai de réinterprétation
des positions thomistes" in *Le péché de l'Ange*, 59.

our topic, in the *De malo*, when an objector to Thomas' teaching intervenes to foreground the distinctiveness of the supernatural and to enquire whether that natural/ supernatural distinction might mean the whole discussion should be reconceived. So much for the first "moment" in the angel's beginning.

The angel's "beginning" also comprises, however, a second "moment" when it first starts to exercise its own created will. That free deployment of love (or hate) cannot be avoided by appeal to the superlative quality of the angel's intelligence. Whatever may be, in the Jesuit Thomist Pierre Rousselot's famous phrase, "the intellectualism of St. Thomas," this is not it![7] The angel's "determination" of its own act draws on its supreme resources of intelligence, yes. But up to that point, it is simply expressing the "inclinations or dynamisms" grasped as the good proportionate to its nature. The angel is still required to pass from determination (or *specification*) to *exercise* where it acts freely, and thus for better or worse, in terms of its own (natural and supernatural) goal.

Neither the structure of the angel's psychology nor the "metaphysical structure of its destiny"[8] requires it to embrace in full amplitude its own proper finality. In Guérard's austere and distinctive language, there is the "possibility of under-specification of the connatural good *as end*" (the emphasis is original).[9] The distinction between nature and supernature remains pertinent to the enquiry

---

7   Gilliot, 535: "This acknowledgment of the autonomy of free exercise clears Thomas of any suspicion of intellectualism, if by intellectualism we mean a necessary connection between intellectual apprehension of the good and voluntary choice." — "Cette autonomie reconnue à la liberté d'exercice permet de laver Thomas de tout soupçon d'intellectualisme, si on entend par intellectualisme un enchaînement nécessitant entre la saisie intellectuelle du bien et le choix volontaire."

8   To cite a phrase from H.-F. Dondaine, one of the "classical" Dominican Thomists Guérard was opposing.

9   Guérard, 34: "possibilité d'hypo-spécification du bien connaturel *comme fin*."

(the "dramatic transition"), since the "act of free option in the second moment coincides with the act of charity by which God is preferentially loved with a supernatural love," and yet the "action of the free will has a genuine consistency independently of its elevation by grace." Thus are the claims of Position B vindicated, without exploding what is just in the claims of Position A.

And just as Guérard's treatment of the sin of the angel has shown how Thomas' texts may suitably be harmonized, and, in so doing, has enlightened us as to their (both Guérard's and Thomas') stance on the question of nature and the supernatural (the supernatural, in Guérard's Scheeben-esque phrase, by an "intimate marriage with nature in each of its ontological determinations exalts it"[10]), so here it opens up a new possibility for an enrichment of the Thomist tradition in something of the way that was hoped for in the 1950s discussion of the threats and promises posed by *nouvelle théologie*. From the point Guérard has reached, the subjectivity of the angel can stand in for the subjectivity of any person—including that of each member of the human race. As Gilliot puts it, although the will is under a moral obligation in regard to its end in the line of *specification*, "the self-determination of the will in its *exercise* assures for each person a unique fashion of carrying himself towards his own end" (emphasis ours).[11]

Borrowing a key phrase from contemporary French theologian Emmanuel Durand, freedom is a "power of singularization of the subject."[12] The "adventure" of angelic freedom exhibits angelic personhood; the same is true of our own.

When freedom morphs from a reality of our common spiritual nature to a (further) reality of our unique

10 *Ibid.*, 26.
11 Gilliot, 535: "quoique normée par la spécification, l'autodétermination de la volonté dans son exercice assure pour chaque personne une façon unique de se porter vers sa fin."
12 Emmanuel Durand, *L'être humain, divin appel. Anthropologie et création* (Paris : Éditions du Cerf, 2016) 249.

personhood, the *lacunae* of the *philosophia perennis* on the topic of personal singularity can be filled. The writing of Augustine's *Confessions,* when combined with the African Doctor's enormous standing in the West, might have achieved this by highlighting the importance of the personal in its narrative, biographical, unfolding—and thus in its creative inhabiting of historical setting in each individual's life-situation. The *haecceitas* of Scotus sought, with inadequate metaphysical tools, to do our uniqueness justice. Edith Stein came closer: in the words of English Catholic writers of our own day, John and Anna Rist, in their co-authored 2023 *Confusion in the West,* "Stein came to understand that human beings cannot be summed up 'without remainder' as members of a numbered set; we need more serious *metaphysical* reflection on the first person aspects of each human individual."[13] Not for nothing is their study sub-titled *Retrieving Tradition in the Modern and Post-Modern World.* Serendipitously fulfilling the hopes of Teresa Benedicta of the Cross, Guérard des Lauriers showed how best to do just that.

---

13   Anna Rist and John Rist, *Confusion in the West: Retrieving Tradition in the Modern and Post-Modern World,* (Cambridge: Cambridge University Press, 2022) 223.

"The Joy without a Cause"

NOTES ON CHESTERTON'S BALLAD OF THE WHITE HORSE

VINCENT-MARY HOARE, FSVF

GILBERT KEITH CHESTERTON (1874–1936) is best known as a novelist and Christian controversialist, but in fact, after thirty years of reading this "Defender of the Catholic Faith," as Pius XI called him, I now find his best and deepest works in his poetry.

There are poems about Our Lady, about Christ, about politics ... some are simply fun poems, perhaps intended for an evening of mirth with his friends Belloc and Baring, but there is always a message of wisdom behind his madness. Take the one about drink, for instance, called "Wine and Water":

> Old Noah he had an ostrich farm...
> ... where everything the Patriarch took on board was on an absolutely enormous scale,
> And the soup he took was Elephant Soup and the fish he took was Whale,
> But they all were small to the cellar he took when he set out to sail,
> And Noah he often said to his wife when he sat down to dine,
> I don't care where the water goes if it doesn't get into the wine.[1]

---

1 *The Collected Poems of G. K. Chesterton*, 7th edition (London: Methuen & Co, 1939), 200. All subsequent quotations are cited from this collection.

THE *BALLAD OF THE WHITE HORSE*

One of his poetic works stands out by reason of its epic style and length: 2,684 lines divided into eight books—over two hours to read aloud.[2] The *Ballad of the White Horse*, completed in 1911, is apparently the only published poem that Chesterton dedicated to his wife.[3] It takes us to pre-Norman England, to the stories of Alfred in ninth century which seem like "the tales a whole tribe feigns, too English to be true."[4] After the Danish invasions, the whole island is under the domination of this utterly barbarian, savage people who pillage and massacre. The Saxon King of Wessex, Alfred, is powerless before Guthrum, the Danish king. Poet and literary critic Malcolm Guite writes:

> This great poem is as much about modern times as it is a ballad of the days of King Alfred. In 1911 Chesterton foresaw that the modern Nihilism and worship of the "superman" embodied in the writings of Nietzsche together with false worship of race and a cult of violence, would likely wreak unimaginable damage in the new century, as proved to be the case. He also saw that a renewal of the vision of joy and humility that is at the heart of the Christian creed was the only way to resist the death-wish which is the shadow side of our fallen humanity. He wrote a poem at whose heart is a call to courage kindled not by probable chances of success but by what he called 'the joy without a cause.'[5]

---

2   A recording of the *Ballad of the White Horse* by Br. Vincent-Mary is accessible at: https://www.youtube.com/@praywithneums.
3   Maisie Ward, *Gilbert Keith Chesterton* (New York: Sheed & Ward, 1943), 245, writes: "The poem is a ballad in the sense of the old ballads that were stirring stories: it is also an expression of the threefold love of Gilbert's life: his wife, his country and his faith. And, as in all great poetry, there is a quality of eternity in this poem that has made it serve as an expression of the eternal spirit of man."
4   *The Collected Poems*, 222.
5   Malcolm Guite, "The Ballad of the White Horse: a complete reading for King Alfred's Day," 26 October 2020, available at: https://

The White Horse is an enormous figure carved in chalk on a hillside in Oxfordshire, dating from prehistoric times, perhaps from the Bronze Age. In the Ballad it seems to represent the endless past, traditions lost in time—it is what each generation inherits without fully understanding why. Despite its pagan origins, this monument is an emblem worthy of respect. "For the White Horse knew England when there was none to know."[6] It is noteworthy that since the time of the conversion of England under the Celtic saints, and later under St. Augustine of Canterbury, this great figure was preserved by a healthy instinct to respect traditions. By contrast, as we shall see, Chesterton depicts the Danes despising such things, believing instead in gods of meaningless destruction.

I shall focus on a few episodes only, hoping this may encourage some people to read and enjoy this wonderful poem for themselves.

THE JOY WITHOUT A CAUSE

King Alfred is in a completely desperate situation. His people are half-starved and clothed in rags, while he lives on a river island. Although he has the impression that God has abandoned him, he keeps his faith. As Alfred calls to mind a childhood memory of his mother showing him an illuminated prayer book, Our Lady appears to him. But her message is not quite what one would expect. In answer to the king's gesture of throwing his most precious jewel (known today as the Alfred Jewel) at her feet and expressing his great fear of the gates of heaven, Our Lady, whose voice is "like a belfry burst in song," says:

> The gates of heaven are lightly locked,
> We do not guard our gain...
> And any little maid that walks

---

malcolmguite.wordpress.com/2020/10/26/the-ballad-of-the-white-horse-a-complete-reading-for-king-alfreds-day-2/ (last accessed 27 February 2024).
6   *The Collected Poems*, 225.

> In good thoughts apart,
> May break the guard of the Three Kings
> And see the dear and dreadful things
> I hid within my heart.[7]

She goes on to promise him nothing, except that things are going to get worse.

> I tell you naught for your comfort,
> Yea, naught for your desire,
> Save that the sky grows darker yet
> And the sea rises higher.
>
> Night shall be thrice night over you
> And heaven an iron cope.
> Do you have joy without a cause,
> Yea, faith without a hope?[8]

This joy is what fires Alfred into action. "The joy without a cause" becomes his leitmotif. (This verbal interplay is typical of Chesterton, and my impression is that he is playing with the words *joy* and *cause*. The cause of Christian joy is our infinitely good God, and the vision seems to be saying: you have a great cause for joy. But God is infinite Joy, and is of course uncaused; He is thus Joy without a cause. So Alfred, in having Christ in his heart, possesses Joy without a cause. The same phrase is thus charged with meaning.)

King Alfred proceeds to muster his men, and there follows a colorful description of Eldred, Mark, and Colan, three types who make up the England Alfred will found.

Eldred is your good, hearty, powerfully built countryman, who is persuaded to leave his plums and take up his rusty sword again. *Mark* represents Roman organization and power, but he also complies, for each time it is the account of Our Lady's words that is the deciding factor for joining Alfred. Then you have *Colan* the Irishman, and our poet goes to town about the character of his rain-wrapped isle:

---

7   *Ibid.*, 231.
8   *Ibid.*, 233.

> For the great Gaels of Ireland
> Are the men that God made mad,
> For all their wars are merry,
> And all their songs are sad.[9]

(Chesterton, who loved Ireland, is always very amusing about the Irish, and the French for that matter.) Ultimately, Colan, too, only accepts to fight with Alfred's "army of eastland yokels," as he calls them, because of the King's vision.

SINGING AROUND THE CAMPFIRE

A particularly interesting episode takes place on the vigil of the attack, in Book III. Alfred goes to the camp of the Danes disguised as a wandering harpist. The chief Danes each sing a song. Chesterton manages in these five songs to express a great deal about the human heart, about belief and disbelief.

Alfred starts the round by singing of "some old British raid ... of war in the warm wet shires," but he is soon interrupted by Harold, the young nephew of King Guthrum, who, snatching the instrument, strums away about the Viking triumphs of world domination and spoliation: "We shall enjoy the world, the whole huge world a toy."[10] He goes on to mock the Brits' wimpy religion; they have been "turned to women by the god of the nails from Rome." Harold's song is thus "the song of the Thief of the World and the gods that loved the thief."[11] Even King Guthrum finds this distasteful, and invites Elf the Germanic minstrel to continue. Elf, who is from "the land of the folk-songs" where "the tears come easily," sings about the sad insecurity of love, but it is sinister to note that "the heart of each man moved in him like a babe buried alive."[12]

---

9   Ibid., 242.
10 Ibid., 248.
11 Ibid.
12 Ibid., 249.

The third Viking leader, the older warrior Earl Ogier, plucks the harp in stark contrast to what has gone before. Elf has sung "of the young gods easily," but there are "gods behind the gods, gods which are best unsung." Now why sing about something which is best kept quiet? Ogier goes on to reveal "the wrath of the gods who would rend all gods and men," and "who are weary to make an end," and he ends by mocking heaven itself, "the happy town," for "hate alone is true."[13] Here is an image of pure evil, a man possessed by hatred for everything.

Again, Guthrum cannot quite stomach such an attitude: "not all things would I rend," and "it is best to abide the end" to see if life be good or bad. Guthrum's turn has come, but he sings wearily, because "the truth is cold to tell"; the body is "a broken shell" and the soul is "like a lost bird" that, when at last found, is discovered dead. In despair he admits to wasting the world in vain, because everything and everyone, including the gods themselves, end miserably in death. "A tear is in the tiniest flower because the gods must die."[14]

It seems to me that these four songs embody four distinct anti-Christian philosophies:

1) Harold's "enjoy life for yourself and despise others": pure self-love;

2) Elf's conviction that love, though it does exist, is doomed to be perpetually unstable, i.e., a denial of eternal perfect love;

3) Ogier's will to destroy absolutely everything, creation, oneself and God: pure hatred of the Creator;

4) Guthrum's "forget your soul because it's dead anyway": despair.

Alfred is thus somewhat outnumbered and outweighed. But this is central to Chesterton's theme; the Christian is a most surprising entity, for he is actually at his best

---

13   *Ibid.*, 252.
14   *Ibid.*, 253.

when he is placed in an utterly hopeless position. This
is what makes the *Ballad* so poignant today.

Alfred takes up the harp again, as it falls from Guthrum's hands, but his musical style has quite changed since
Harold's intervention, for "his stroke had all the rattle and
spark of horses flying hard." He will now make answer
why Wessex men "be meek and monkish folk and bow to
the White Lord's broken yoke": "Our monks go robed in
rain and snow, but the heart of flame therein, but you go
clothed in feasts and flames, when all is ice within"—"On
you is fallen the shadow, and not upon the Name"—"What
have the strong gods given?"—"I know what spirit with
whom you blindly band hath blessed destruction with his
hand." And finally:

> Ere the sad gods that made your gods
> Saw their sad sunrise pass,
> The White Horse of the White Horse Vale,
> That you have left to darken and fail,
> Was cut out of the grass.
>
> Therefore your end is on you,
> Is on you and your kings,
> Not for a fire in Ely fen...
> But because it is only Christian men
> Guard even heathen things.
>
> For our God hath blessed creation,
> Calling it good...[15]

The Vikings are all-powerful for the moment, "all
lances split on you, all swords be heaved in vain," but
yet Christian men "have more lust again to lose than
you to win again."[16]

They laugh him to scorn as he leaves in the twilight,
for their disbelief has no answer to his vibrant confidence
in Christ.

---

15   *Ibid.*, 256-57.
16   *Ibid.*, 256.

THE BATTLE OF ETHANDUNE

Now, let us turn our attention to Book V, the battle-field of Ethandune.

The Wessex army is really like a troop of tramps in rags against fierce and masterful men of war on horseback with horned helmets and colorful livery. Nevertheless, the beginning of the battle is rather spectacular, and that thanks to the Irish flank.

The interaction between the two armies begins with Harold, the conceited nephew of King Guthrum, who boasts that these scarecrows are scarcely worth fighting:

> Meeting may be of war-men,
> Where the best war-man wins;
> But all this carrion a man shoots
> Before the fight begins.[17]

And so he takes up a hunter's bow at random and aims at the Irishman. But Colan, fast as lightening, throws his sword spinning through the air at Harold's forehead. Here Chesterton, like the poets of the ancient epics, can really delve into the gory details of war, yet without descending to morbidity; he is acknowledging the fact that we are flesh and blood, that our bodies also have to be used at times to defend ourselves and the honor of God.

To my mind, we have here the animating idea behind Chesterton's poem. As in many of his books, we here witness a great, big battle between good and evil. And the good are very, very nearly defeated. Then, at the last minute, the tide turns. And this is highly realistic of him, because real life frequently displays this same pattern; whether you like it or not, and whether you believe it or not, each generation and each individual walks a tightrope between victory and defeat, salvation and damnation. A man must not stick his head in the sand like an ostrich and ignore the terrible battle being waged at his flanks!

---

17 *Ibid.*, 277.

Alfred and his men are of course defeated and driven
back, his thanes Eldred and Mark having been respectively
pierced through by the bewitched spear of Elf and stabbed
to death by Ogier's hateful hand. The Irish retreat down
one road where Colan is killed, and the Wessex men are
forced down another road, this separation of their forces
proving catastrophic.

Alfred, whose character as a leader shines forth in
this dreadful hour, sounds the horn to stop the hopeless
retreat and muster the wretched survivors, for only the
poor are left, his best warriors all dead. It is these poor
survivors and Hildred the hedge cutter, Gurth the hunter
and Gorlias the sailor, who heroically reform in a pathetic
line to charge and "go to God."

At this point Alfred simply raises his eyes to heaven—
what else can he do? And then, when all is lost and the
last arrow flown, he sees a great light "like death":

> For Our Lady stood on the standards rent,
> As lonely and as innocent,
> As when between white walls she went
> And the lilies of Nazareth.
> Her eyes were sad withouten art,
> And seven swords were in her heart—

And then comes the striking verse: "But one was in
her hand."[18] Traditional iconography represents Our Lady
of the Seven Sorrows with seven swords piercing her
heart, but here in this great Ballad one of them is in
her beautiful hand.

> And she was a queen most womanly—
> But she was a queen of men.

(Since when have Catholics belittled womanhood?) Now
quite suddenly the whole situation has changed:

> The high tide! King Alfred cried.
> The high tide and the turn![19]

---

18   *Ibid.*, 297.
19   *Ibid.*, 298.

—apparently this was the quotation used for the *Times* headlines in Britain after the D-Day landings[20]—

> The Mother of God goes over them,
> On dreadful Cherubs borne;
> And the psalm is roaring above the rune . . .[21]

It is stirring stuff as Alfred at last and against all the odds gains the upper hand. As the Danes are routed, Alfred continues:

> The Mother of God goes over them,
> Walking on wind and flame . . .
> And the White Horse stamps in the White Horse Vale,
> And we shall yet drink Christian ale
> In the village of our name.

THE PROPHECY OF MODERN PAGANS

In the eighth and last book of the Ballad, Wessex is at peace. Alfred has driven the Danes into the eastern part of England and King Guthrum has converted to Christianity. The book is called "The Scouring of the Horse" because keeping the horse scoured of moss and weeds becomes a kind of symbol of keeping the Faith

---

20 Cf. Malcolm Guite, "The Ballad of the White Horse: a complete reading for King Alfred's Day." See also: Maisie Ward, *Gilbert Keith Chesterton*, 285–86: "During the First World War, many soldiers had it with them in the trenches. 'I want to tell you,' the widow of a sailor wrote 'that a copy of *The Ballad of the White Horse* went down into the Humber with the R.38. My husband loved it as his own soul—never went anywhere without it.'" Newspapers also quoted it at key points in the Second World War. After the disaster of Crete in 1941, writes Ward, "the *Times* had the shortest first leader in its history. Under the heading *Sursum Corda* was a brief statement of the disaster followed by the words of Our Lady to King Alfred. *I tell you nought for your comfort . . . Do you have joy without a cause? / Yea, faith without a hope?* The unbreakable strength of that apparently faint and tenuous thread of faith appeared in the sequel. [. . .] Months later [in November 1942], when Winston Churchill spoke of 'the end of the beginning,' the *Times* returned to the White Horse and gave the opening of Alfred's speech at Ethandune: *The high tide! King Alfred cried. / The high tide and the turn!*"

21 *The Collected Poems*, 299.

unadulterated. But Alfred foresees the coming of pagans
in the future:

> Though I give this land to Our Lady...
> I know that weeds shall grow in it
> Faster than men can burn...
> In some far century, sad and slow,
> I have a vision, and I know
> The heathen shall return.

In the verses that follow, one feels Chesterton almost
at a loss as to how to describe the subversive nature of
these future pagans:

> Yea, this shall be the sign of them,
> The sign of the dying fire;
> And Man made like a half-wit,
> That knows not of his sire...
>
> Accursed from the beginning,
> By detail of the sinning,
> And denial of the sin;
>
> By thought a crawling ruin,
> By life a leaping mire,
> By a broken heart in the breast of the world,
> And the end of the world's desire;
>
> By God and man dishonoured,
> By death and life made vain,
> Know ye the old barbarian,
> The barbarian come again...
>
> In what wise men shall smite him,
> Or the Cross stand up again,
> Or charity or chivalry,
> My vision saith not.[22]

The Ballad thus ends on a somewhat foreboding note.
The vision cuts off here because surely the rest depends
on Chesterton's audience; it was published in 1911, just
three years before World War I began. Although Alfred

---

22   *Ibid.*, 313–314.

goes on to take London town after a second Danish invasion, he does so full of doubts about the future, and the Ballad depicts a backdrop of the White Horse becoming a prey to weeds.

In this epic work of *The Ballad of The White Horse*, Alfred is portrayed as a key example for our times. In his dedication to the poem, Chesterton had emphasized that this is "no fairy tale." Far from being better than the bloody ninth century, our times are surely those of this final vision; indeed, today's Vikings with their gods of Wokeism, infanticide, suicide and gender juggling, seem all-powerful and predominant, but their time is up, for "the gods must die."[23]

For the moment, "they ruin and make dark,"[24] but we must, like Alfred the Great, keep the "joy without a cause" and be ready to make the final charge and go to God, confident that the Mother of God watches over us and can intervene any moment.

---

23 *Ibid.*, 253.
24 *Ibid.*, 313.

Book Reviews

Thomas Crean, O. P.
COMMENTARY ON THE GOSPEL OF ST. MARK
(Waterloo, ON: Arouca Press, 2022), 141 pp.

This short commentary on St. Mark's Gospel seeks a return to biblical exegesis that nourishes the faithful in heart and in mind. Each chapter follows the Douai-Rheims translation on the left-hand side, with a corresponding commentary mirrored on the opposite page. As the householder, "who bringeth forth out of his treasure new things and old" (Mt. 13:52), Fr. Thomas Crean shares the Church's rich tradition with the reader. This volume displays the same qualities as the same author's *Commentary on St. Luke's Gospel*, although certain passages of this Gospel have been left unadorned, out of a desire to avoid treading over the same ground as his previous commentary. Fr. Crean does not shy away from those uncomfortable truths or difficult passages which can be found in the Evangelist's words, but rather confronts them with a measured caution. In suggesting many spiritual or speculative interpretations of the Gospel, the work leaves open many threads to be more deeply investigated and meditated upon by the reader, at his own pace.

Readers of St. Thomas will perhaps recognize that this commentary seems inspired by the exegetical method used by the Angelic Doctor. Fr. Crean draws out the literal sense of the text, with its historical and theological dimensions, and he also enters into its allegorical sense. Moreover, like his medieval predecessors, Fr. Crean assumes the truth of the early tradition that St. Mark drew his Gospel from the preaching of St. Peter at Rome. Special attention is given to the many places where St. Mark adds some detail or vivid touch that is unique to himself. As a foretaste of Fr. Crean's exegetical method, let us give two examples:

> Chap. 1, 12–13: *And immediately the Spirit drove him out into the desert. And he was in the desert forty days and forty nights, and was tempted by Satan; and he was with beasts, and the angels ministered to him.*
>
> Commentary: Does the Holy Spirit have authority over Christ, since He *drove him out into the wilderness*? In His humanity, Christ was subject to the Holy Spirit; but this verse refers especially to the intense charity of His human soul, infused by the Holy Ghost, by which He was impelled to go to the wilderness to pray and fast for mankind. Only St. Mark mentions *the wild beasts* who were with Him there. Abba Paul of the Thebaid, one of the desert Fathers, said: "If a man has obtained purity, everything is in submission to him, as it was to Adam when he was in Paradise before he transgressed." How much more were these beasts tame toward Christ, the new Adam.
>
> Chap. 14, 22: *and whilst they were eating Jesus took bread; and blessing it, broke it, and gave to them, and said: Take ye. This is my body.*
>
> Commentary: [W]e may suppose that the short form of words pronounced over the bread, lacking the words 'given for you' quoted by Saint Luke and Saint Paul, reflects the practice of the Roman church over which Saint Peter presided; the Roman rite of mass, as far back as we can trace it, lacked these words, unlike the Eastern rites, which contained them.

Thus this commentary opens the door of the Sacred Scriptures, be it for those who have not yet commenced this study, or for those whose established practice of *lectio divina* might benefit from the light of those who have gone before us in the Faith.

P. V.

William of Tocco
THE LIFE OF ST. THOMAS AQUINAS
Translated with an Introduction by Dr. David Foley,
and a Foreword by Fr. Thomas Crean, O. P.
(St. Marys, KS: Angelus Press, 2023), 227 pp.

In 1959, Kenelm Foster, O. P., published *The Life of Saint Thomas Aquinas: Biographical Documents*, which included early accounts of the saint's life by Bernard Gui, Tolomeo of Lucca, and others. Despite his continuous reliance on William of Tocco's *Ystoria*, Foster chose not to include this earliest and fullest account of the Angelic Doctor's life in his volume due to considerations of "taste and convenience." In Foster's estimation, Tocco "is tediously and conventionally rhetorical ... It is Tocco's rhetoric that makes him a bore."[1] It has been 65 years since Foster offered this questionable and admittedly subjective defense of his choice to deprive the English-reading world of the opportunity to access this crucial primary source on the life of St. Thomas. For the seventh centenary of the Angelic Doctor's canonization, Dr. David Foley has remedied this deficit by offering us an eloquent translation of this foundational work.

In his instructive introduction to the translation, Foley prepares us to encounter the so-called tedium of Tocco's opus by pointing out that it resembles *lectio divina*: "first, he [Tocco] examines the literal course of events in Thomas' life (*lectio*); he then meditates upon the spiritual realities hidden in these events, as he relates them to the revealed truths of Scripture (*meditatio*); finally, his meditation culminates in moments of contemplative prayer (*contemplatio*), as we glimpse in his rhetorical invocations of the saint at the end of certain chapters."[2] Foley emphasizes that we should not expect a modern biographical account of Thomas' life in chronological sequence, but a thematically

---

1   Kenelm Foster, O. P., *The Life of St. Thomas Aquinas: Biographical Documents* (London: Longmans, Green & Co., 1959), 9.
2   David M. Foley, "Translator's Introduction," in *William of Tocco: The Life of St. Thomas Aquinas*, 19.

ordered hagiographical portrait of a man of God who exemplifies the virtues of the heroes of salvation history. Even those portions of the text that follow a chronological sequence, particularly the account of St. Thomas' early life, are concerned to show that the life of St. Thomas was patterned on the Scriptures he so dearly loved to expound and meditate on. St. Thomas' early life, like that of Jesus Christ himself, is marked by the prophecy of his birth and greatness (The Annunciation), his deliverance as an infant from a natural disaster that did not spare his sister (Slaughter of the Innocents), and his youthful precociousness as an oblate in seeking answers about the nature of God (The Child Jesus in the Temple). The early, more chronological part of the work is completed by a chapter (16) devoted to showing St. Thomas's similarity to Isaac, Jacob, Moses, and Solomon as if to emphasize that the full living out of the Christian life simply is the living out of the patterns of holiness God has set before us in the sacred pages. From this point until the account of St. Thomas' death, Tocco is much more interested in spiritual themes than in chronological accuracy.

Thomas Crean, O. P., in his insightful foreword, highlights the salient themes Tocco wants us to be attentive to. First, there is St. Thomas' absolute commitment to religious life as illustrated in his perseverance through his two-year captivity by his family and unwavering discipline in following the Dominican rule. Second, St. Thomas' devotion to the truth of God is a continuous thread from his youth to his death and is most vividly illustrated by the descriptions of St. Thomas' reliance on God in coming to know the truth. Third, the virtue St. Thomas displayed in communicating the truth to others is effectively described in recounting his ability to counter error and heresy with equanimity, humility, and charity. Most remarkable to this reader, however, are the observations Tocco makes about St. Thomas' preaching and discourse in Chapter 48. There, the biographer notes that St. Thomas' preaching was suited not to the erudite, but to the simple, and that all his concern was to converse with and about God. Tocco finishes the chapter: "In some way, the circuit of heaven was encompassed within him, for in prayer Thomas set his mind into motion, proceeding from himself towards God, and in teaching this motion was completed by moving from God towards his neighbor; then again, by prayer and contemplation, this motion was enkindled from within him towards God, and thus did he renew the heavenly course."[3] If this is an example of Tocco's supposedly tedious rhetoric, I hope to be forgiven for my lack of urbanity for finding it delightful, as it calls to mind the famed *exitus-reditus* structure of St. Thomas' two great *Summae*. If the life of the saints on earth is but a prelude to heaven, a more apt description of such a life is difficult to be found.

Having struggled to some extent with Tocco's Latin, it is a pleasure to read such a lucid translation of such difficult prose. Perhaps Foster was correct to judge Tocco's Latinity affected; my own formation in the Church's vernacular does not permit me to make such a judgment. Foley's English, however, is elegant without being elaborate. On occasion, he makes use of archaic language, particularly when translating prayers. This may be off-putting for some readers, but it certainly does not hinder ready understanding of the text. He has included useful notes throughout for readers unfamiliar with the debates St. Thomas engaged in, medieval university customs, Dominican traditions, literary and historical features of the text, and the like; these are geared more to the intelligent non-expert than to scholars of Thomistic thought. Academics who want greater detail would be better served by turning to the Latin critical edition of the text or the French translation thereof, both authored by Claire le Brun-Gouanvic, whose fine scholarship Foley regularly draws upon.

---

3   *Ibid.*, 168.

While those familiar with scholarly works on the life of St. Thomas, like those of Weisheipl and Torrell, will be largely familiar with the stories in this text, it is a pleasure to finally have a readily accessible volume of the work on which those great scholars so heavily relied. As Crean notes in the foreword, Tocco's account is well supplemented by recourse to other texts, such as those supplied by Foster in his indispensable volume. Nevertheless, for lovers of primary sources, Foley's translation is a most welcome addition to the corpus of texts on the life of the Angelic Doctor. Angelus Press has done a fine job in producing a handsome, affordable, and seemingly very durable hardcover book. The binding is too tight to have the book remain open when set down, but not so tight that one worries about breaking the spine when opening it wide. Though the cover art is lovely, lovelier still would be an additional dust jacket to protect the hardcover from nicks and scratches.

Following directly upon this edition of Tocco, Angelus Press has just issued another fine volume of previously untranslated medieval Latin works, Pope Innocent III's *The Mysteries of the Mass* and *The Four Kinds of Marriage*, likewise translated with an introduction by Foley and featuring a foreword by Dr. Peter Kwasniewski. It is my hope that these publications signal a renewed movement on the part of traditional Catholic publishers to give English readers wider access to our medieval Latin patrimony, which would indeed meet with the enthusiasm of scholars and laymen alike.

Charles Robertson, Ph.D.
(University of St. Thomas, Houston, TX)
St. Thérèse Institute of Faith
and Mission, Bruno, SK

An Episode from the Infancy of the Angelic Doctor

DRAWN FROM WILLIAM OF TOCCO'S *LIFE OF ST. THOMAS AQUINAS* (1323)

WILLIAM OF TOCCO'S *LIFE OF St. Thomas Aquinas was first published 700 years ago for the Angelic Doctor's canonization. This text, originally commissioned by the Dominican Order to promote Thomas' cause and composed by the saint's younger confrere, is the first biography of St. Thomas and the foundation of all subsequent studies of his life. It was translated into English for the first time by Dr. David Foley and published by Angelus Press in 2023. The following chapter is reproduced from this edition with the kind permission of the Press.*

On a scrap of parchment containing the salutation to the Blessed Virgin, which the child found by divine Providence and refused to let go.

OTHER EVENTS THROUGHOUT THE infancy of this child seem to have presaged the divine Grace that was to follow, and these I consider worthy to be preserved in memory and recorded indelibly in the written word. Once, it happened that the boy's mother went to the city of Naples, her birthplace, to visit the public baths with other noblewomen, while the nurse brought her son along. When the nurse set him down in the spot where children normally sat at the baths, the boy found a piece of parchment that was providentially lying there, and he tottered over to pick it up, although no one told him to do so. Now when the nurse wished to undress him and open the hand in which he was holding the parchment, the boy raised a piercing cry. Being moved by pity, the nurse consented to bathe, dry, and dress the child, who kept his hand tightly closed all the while, and she brought him back to the house in this same fashion alongside the boy's mother. Finally, when his mother managed to pry open the infant's hand—though he wailed fiercely at her doing—she discovered there a little scrap of parchment containing nothing other than the words *Ave Maria*, the angelic salutation to the glorious Virgin. This was a sign worthy of divine Providence: what was here foreshadowed in the infant would be accomplished hereafter by the Master of Theology. It was indeed fitting that this boy, under no other guidance than that of the Holy Spirit, should find a parchment containing the first stroke of our salvation, the same salutary doctrine that he was destined to elucidate in his manhood.

From this time on it became the child's extraordinary habit—one instilled by divine inspiration rather than acquired by repeated behaviour—that whenever he began to cry for any reason, he would not be comforted by any of his nurse's coddling until he could lay hold on a piece of parchment. Immediately after he received one, he would put it into his mouth. By this, it seemed to be divinely foreshown that the boy's discerning rumination upon the Scriptures would precede everything that he set out in writing. Beyond this, we can see what a pure savor he would later find in his studies as a doctor, and what sweet fruits he would lay out for others in his writing. Such, too, is the wonderful knowledge that the divine wisdom implants in the bee: all of the honeyed words of divine science, which he would collect from the lovely flowers of Sacred Scripture in the swift flight of his studies, he

gathered up into the honeycomb of his books, sealing them
there by the word of his most learned mouth, from thence
to be extracted for the delight of the entire Church. Just
as Ezekiel was commanded, so too was the book given
to this child for food by the hand of an angel, which
he chewed upon for the wisdom of contemplation (Ezek.
3:3); he consumed everything that he found there by the
swiftness of his learning, even as it was said of John in
the Apocalypse (Apoc. 10:9). In this way, the true meaning must be distinguished from the letter in the book of
the Old Law by rumination, while in the New Law the
divine mysteries of the Faith have been made manifest,
as though to be consumed directly by the mouth of the
soul. As a doctor who was thoroughly instructed in these
matters, Thomas was able to perceive so profoundly the
truths of the Old Law, as if by consuming them, and to
demonstrate the truths of the New Law to others, as if
for them to consume, with such clarity that he seemed
to be infused with light.

This book of apologetics stands in a tradition going back to the earliest days of the Church, and which includes such luminaries as St Augustine, Pascal, and Cardinal Newman. It sets forth reasons for belief in a clear, attractive and convincing way. As such, it should be appreciated by any open-minded and honest enquirer.

Translated by
Fr. Thomas Crean, O.P.

Christianity
IS
CREDIBLE

LOUIS-MARIE DE BLIGNIÈRES, FSVF
Translated by Thomas Crean, OP

186 pages

The work of commending the Gospels for their historical credibility may seem pedestrian in the eyes of a theologian. But the ordinary person, if they have an enquiring mind, will see in it an absolutely essential task. I expect *Christianity is Credible* to prove a very useful apologetic text.

- *Aidan Nichols, O.P., author of Criticising the Critics: Catholic Apologias for Today*

At a time when the understanding of truth is muddled, Fr. Crean's translation of *Christianity is Credible* by Fr. de Blignières upholds the perennial standard of the Church that rejects both fideism and rationalism. Fr. de Blignières' work of apologetics dives into depths of divine revelation with the anchor of natural reason, hence uniting supernatural faith with our God-given reason. By addressing the pivotal claims of Christianity in clarity and pith, this book provides an unmatched account of the birth of our Faith.

- *Derya Little, author of From Islam to Christ: One Woman's Path through the Riddles of God*

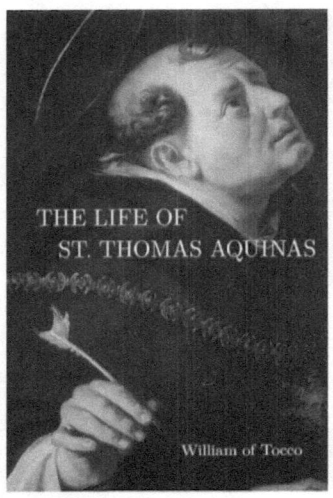

THE MYSTERIES OF THE MASS
THE FOUR KINDS OF MARRIAGE

The Mysteries of the Mass and The Four Kinds
of Marriage were written in 1196 and 1197 and
represent some of the best of Catholic
philosophy, theology, and biblical exegesis of the
medieval period. In these works Pope Innocent
provides an answer to modern society's most
pivotal questions.

This beautifully bound, intellectually gripping
volume belongs in the homes of Catholic families,
liturgists, theologians, and students of the
humanities throughout the English-speaking
world. It is a timeless Catholic classic that is sure
to ground your knowledge of the faith while
introducing you to one of the brightest minds to
have occupied throne of St. Peter.

It is published in English for the first time in
history by Angelus Press and translated by
David Foley.
Hardback, 327 pp.

THE LIFE OF
ST. THOMAS AQUINAS

"All who desire to know Saint Thomas personally
would do well to read this striking account of his
life." —Fr. Paul Robinson

While most Catholics are familiar with the
writings of St. Thomas Aquinas, little is known
about the saint himself... until now. This insightful
biography of St. Thomas Aquinas appears for the
first time in English after its composition seven
centuries ago.

This book gives a charming eyewitness account of
the unseen life of St. Thomas Aquinas and helps
us better understand the family, friends, and era
that produced one of the greatest theologians of
all time

This book was used as part of the canonization
process for St. Thomas Aquinas. It is published in
English for the first time in history by Angelus
Press and translated by David Foley.
Hardback, 227 pp.

www.ingramcontent.com/pod-product-compliance
Lightning Source LLC
Chambersburg PA
CBHW021639120626
46545CB00002B/612